*Destination Zero*

BY SAM HAMILL

POETRY

*Heroes of the Teton Mythos*
*Petroglyphs*
*The Calling Across Forever*
*The Book of Elegiac Geography*
*Triada*
*animae*
*Fatal Pleasure*
*The Nootka Rose*
*Passport*
*A Dragon in the Clouds*
*Mandala*
*Destination Zero*

POETRY IN TRANSLATION

*Night Traveling* (from Chinese)
*The Lotus Lovers* (from the Chinese of Tzu Yeh and Li Ch'ing-chao)
*The Same Sea in Us All* (from the Estonian of Jaan Kaplinski)
*Catullus Redivivus* (from the Latin of Catullus)
*The Art of Writing* (from the Chinese of Lu Chi)
*Banished Immortal* (from the Chinese of Li T'ai-po)
*The Wandering Border* (from the Estonian of Jaan Kaplinski)
*Facing the Snow* (from the Chinese of Tu Fu)
*Narrow Road to the Interior* (from the Japanese of Bashō)
*Only Companion* (from Japanese)
*The Infinite Moment* (from Ancient Greek)
*Endless River* (from the Chinese of Tu Fu and Li Po)
*Midnight Flute* (from Chinese)
*The Sound of Water* (from Japanese)

ESSAYS

*At Home in the World*
*Bashō's Ghost*
*A Poet's Work*

EDITOR

*Selected Poems 1938–1988* by Thomas McGrath
*Death Song,* posthumous poems of Thomas McGrath
*Love Poems from the Japanese* by Kenneth Rexroth
*The Erotic Spirit*

# Destination Zero

POEMS 1970–1995

## Sam Hamill

WHITE PINE PRESS

Publication of this book is made possible by grants from the New York State Council on the Arts and the National Endowment for the Arts.

Designed by John D. Berry and Sam Hamill

ISBN 1-877727-53-9 (paper)
ISBN 1-877727-55-5 (cloth)

White Pine Press
10 Village Square
Fredonia, New York 14063

FIRST EDITION
9  8  7  6  5  4  3  2

*Acknowledgments:*

These poems originally appeared in the following journals: *Alaska Quarterly Review, American Poetry Review, Another Chicago Magazine, Catalyst, Cincinnati Poetry Review, Chicago Review, Columbia, Crab Creek Review, Cutbank, Dalmo'ma, Earth First, Hanging Loose, High Country News, Kuksu, Memphis State Review, Midwest Quarterly, Mississippi Mud, Paintbrush, Pequod, Poetry East, Porcupine's Quil, Portland Review, The Ark, Willow Springs, Wind Horse* (Canada) and in the Japanese journals *Sei-en, Kyoto Review, Fune,* and *Blue Jacket.*


Special thanks to the following publishers who have supported my poetry: Three Rivers Press, Carnegie-Mellon University; Bookstore Press; Breitenbush Books; Mildweed Editions; Broken Moon Press.

*for Gray Foster and Eron Hamill*

"The journey itself is home."
– BASHŌ

# Contents

III.

IV.

V.

*Destination Zero*

# A Lover's Quarrel

There are some to whom a place means nothing,
for whom the lazy zeroes
a goshawk carves across the sky
are nothing,
for whom a home is something one can buy.
I have long wanted to say,
just once before I die,
*I am home.*

When I remember the sound of my true country,
I hear winds
high up in the evergreens, the soft snore
of surf, far off, on a wintry day,
the half-garbled song of finches
darting off through alder
on a summer day.

Lust does not
fatigue the soul, I say. This wind,
these ever-
green trees, this little bird of the spirit –
this is the shape, the place of my desire. I'm free
as a fish or a stone.

———

Don't tell me
about the seasons in the East, don't talk to me

about eternal California summer.
It's enough to have
a few days naked
among three hundred kinds of rain.

In its little plastic pot on the high sill,
the African violet
grows away from the place
the sun last was, its fuzzy leaves
leaning out in little curtsies.

It, too, has had enough
of the sun. I love the sound of a storm
without thunder, the way winds
slow, trees darken, heavy clouds
rumbling so softly
you must close your eyes to listen:

then the *blotch, blotch*
of big drops
plunketing through the leaves.

———

It is difficult,
this being a stranger on earth.
Why, I've seen pilgrims come
and tear away at blackberry vines
with everything that's in them, I've seen them
heap their anger
up against a tree

4

and curse these swollen skies.

What's this? – a mountain beaver
no bigger than a newborn mouse
curled in my palm,
an osprey curling over tide pools and lifting
toward the trees, a wind at dusk
hollow in the hollows of the eaves,
a wind over waves
cooling sand crabs washed up along the beach.

Each thing, closely seen,
appears more strange
than before: the shape of my desire
is huge, vague,
full of many things
commingling –

dying bees among the dying flowers;
winter rain and the smoke it brings.

If it fills me with longing,
it is only because we are wind and smoke,
flower and bee;
it is only because
we are like the rain, falling,
falling through our own most secret being,
through a world of not-knowing.

———

At the end of the day,
I come, finally,
to myself, I return to the strange sounds of a man
who wants to speak
with stones, with the hard crust of earth.
But nothing listens.

When the sea hammers the sea wall,
I'm dumb.
When the nighthawks bleat at dusk, I'm drunk
on the sadness of their songs.
When the moon is so close
you can almost reach it through the trees,
I'm frozen, I'm blind,
or I'm gone.

Fish, bird, stone, there's something
I can't know, but know the same:
I hear the rain inside me
only to look up
into a bitter sun.

What do we listen to, what do we think
we hear? The sound
of sea walls crumbling,
a little bird with hunger in its song:
*You should have known! You should have known!*

———

Like any Nootka rose,
I know there are some
for whom a place is nothing. Like the wild rose,
like the tide and the day,
we come, go, or stay
according to a whim.

It is enough, perhaps,
to say, *We live here.*
And let it go at that.

This wind lets go
of everything it touches.
I long to hold the wind.

I'd kiss a fish
and love a stone
and marry the winter rain

if I could persuade this battered earth
to let me make it home.

I.

# *Prolegomenon*

Up all night with a hundred dying chicks
in the jaundiced light of the coop,
my father steps into the first pools of day
pausing at the door to scrape the dung from his boots,
leaning his back to the jamb as he thumbs small
curls of tobacco into the burnt-out bowl of his pipe.

All night his ears rang between the echoes of his heart
with the sickly *cheep, cheep* of small white heads,
mouths agape from twisted necks, beaks drooped open
to ask what no one ever knows, refusing
feed and drink as they died,
twisted in the palm of his hand.

As the sun tears itself open on the blades
of new roofs where orchards he farmed once stood,
he strikes a match, draws deep, and the gray mare
ambles into dew from musky shadows in the barn,
dark tail switching the first flies of the day.
Squinting into the light, a pain too subtle to name

settles into his chest, and as he begin his chores,
morning spreads over him like a stain.

# The Egg

A round yellow light
peeps like a chick
from the round hole
at the end of a round
tin candler at the foot
of the steps in the musk
of a tarpaper cellar.
Six more beams silently break
from tiny holes at the back
which ventilate a bulb
inside. Hunched
in that hint of working light,
my mother candles eggs,
picking each, one by one,
from a basket, holding
each against the light
to look inside for blood
or other signs of life.

A hundred, a thousand eggs
each night, she takes into her hands,
cleans,
examines in the light,
and files in paper cartons
or in cardboard crates.

My father – stubborn, kind –
is out in the dark

of the coops
working like a mule. My mother
thinks of him from egg to egg,
or of her borrowed son.
The work is slow, the light,
'though pale, familiar.

Out in the moonless night,
the cherry tree bursts
into bloom, the first green
waxy shoots of spring break through
her tender crust of topsoil.
Her work, she thinks,
is good: simple and essential.

She cleans and candles
eggs, the pure white eggs
of leghorns, every night,
packing away for sale
the spotless and the sterile,
keeping for her own
the tarnished, the cracked,
and the fertile.

# Dead Letter

Past midnight,
rain driven hard
through trees outside my cabin,
I rise from bed
having slept the sleep without rest,
the strange word still clumsy
on my tongue:

*Father*, I cried from nightmare,
*Father*,

knowing no one was there,
knowing no one ever
would be there,
my own hair graying
and I alone
in another country.

Outside in the wind,
black fists of rain
pummel the night into a bruise
until the stars go out
one after another, and I light
the kerosene lamp
and huddle against the dark.

Father, I say out loud,
awake.

And the wood my own hands
fit and nailed
whispers nothing back.

Twenty years since I left
your house, and thirty
since your large hands
held me up and slipped
me into the saddle.
Your hands were dry and red
as Escalante clay,
and the sweat of a hundred years
ran crazy down
the chiseled ravines of your face.

You told me then
you had more gold in your teeth
than in your bank account,
and laughed
your great bearish laugh
to prove that simple truth.

How many years
since I stooped in the icy mud of winter
above your unmarked grave,
not knowing how to weep,
unable to move,
to speak,

to sigh. A mile north,

where you farmed your life away,
the claws of the angry city
curled into soil,
the soot of all the living
fell from a poisoned sky.

Tonight, by kerosene light,
it all comes back:
after dinner, after evening chores,
when the stoker brims with coal
and with the blood of stewing hens
rinsed from callused hands,

you lean back slow,
eyes closed, and sing
the song of Longfellow's smithy

or the Ballad
of Sam McGee, your voice
as long and dark as Timpanogos Cave.

But the stove that warms these walls
burns wood, and the blood
on my hands
is my own

and cannot be washed away.

I want you
to dry the sweat of long bad dreams,

to show me
how to say the things
I could not say
when I watched your beard
grow long and white
from a thousand miles away.

I blow out the lamp
and listen hard:
only black rain falling forever,

only winds aching in the trees,
only shadows anointing me
with shadows from the past.

Nothing lasts.

Far off,
from the haunted cathedrals
of the narrow human chest, I hear
that old familiar drum
beat out its elegy.

## Letter to Robert Hedin

My Grampa was short and thick and German,
his pock-scarred bulbous nose
usually filled with RoiTan smoke.
What fingers he had were mostly stub:
souvenirs of mines. I remember
how rarely he spoke, how strong
he was, broad shoulders and monk's
straight-as-an-arrow back. He inhabited
an old man's hotel with a lobby
solemn as a mortuary. I rarely went there,
and never to his room. I remember him
among flags and snapdragons
shoveling manure in Ma's old garden.

I write you this not because
you'd have liked him – you would –
but because we are poets: it remains for us
to remember and define. You
who are tall and lean
are like him: quiet, observant,
and intense. All the works and days
of hands with ten full fingers
are at your command. We who have
everything have less: we cuss the silence
and the silence blesses us.

What odd hotels will hold us
when we are old and bones?

In what second-rate retreat
will we learn to lick our wounds
when the roses of desire wither in our skins
and that old friend, agility,
is evicted from our feet. Can we,
you and I, endure those small untimely
everyday defeats old age posits
with earnest, absolute regularity?

Writing this to you, I'm
feeling old already, old enough
for foreign towns and hand-me-down hotels,
thankful for a home-cooked meal,
a letter now and then, true to
the craft to the end, nothing counterfeit
or cruel, thankful to be living,
and for a few wily and durable friends.

## First Snow

The moments that shared us
have divided us
and departed;

no longer the deep fields
remembering our names
written in the rain.

What I have left undone
I leave undone
a white silence

falling through fields
where dark husks
uselessly open.

# Man in the Landscape

I.

Thirty years since I walked
these slow fields of winter,
red-brown snow of Uintah
photographed in sepia,
fence-barbs tipped with frost,
moved among Depression-era faces
mauled by half a century
of working in this weather,

and saw then my first coyote,
an old licorice root
chewed to pieces, a skinny
bit of a thing, hind leg
wired to a fence post,
jaws wired shut,
still half-alive and quivering.

And I heard Old Man Packer –
some claimed he was Albert's brother –
sawed the jaw from another
and set it loose for his dogs,
and laced packets of strychnine
and scattered them in the hills.

And my mother's mother
slept beside her bedpan,
the small bones of each breath

rattling her linen,
and my father wanted
to explain it all away,
but he couldn't.

And in that old brick house
built by my father and mother,
important things went unspoken:
we learned to mourn in silence
and wear a cerement of sweat.

II.
"Nowadays they use ten-eighty,"
the government trapper said.
"Kills a damned sight more'n coyotes.
Put me outta work."

We walked a low knoll
and down a wide sandy path
through patches of chewed grass,
clusters of sage and thistle,
down to the riverbank
to gaze at broad cracks in the mud.

"Found a hawk, red-tail,
up there a ways," he said,
and peered into his hands.
"Dead. And a marten once,
but that was a while back."
He bit a nip from his plug,
chewed, and spit.

22

Then raised his eyes
to the sky. "Mice,
jacks, magpies,... Son-of-a-bitch,
I seen antelope hittin' fences
at fifty miles an hour
and that aint a pretty thing to see.

"This-here's sheep country, boy.
Sheep man is king. My traps
hang on my cabin wall. Shit,
it's gettin' so's any more
a man's got nowhere to go,
he wants to die alone."

III.

Ten-eighty spread on high plains,
TCDD spread all through the forests
where Smohalla asked,
"Would you tear the flesh
from your mother?
Cut her delicate long hair?"

Today a small brown sparrow
crashed into my window
and fell with a broken neck.
It died in my hand.
I set aside my shovel
and walked the D-8 tracks
across a clear-cut slope
where I stopped at a stump
for a smoke.

A blackberry tangle
lay ripped and broken, vines
peeled back, stalks ragged
where metal treads eat land.
Already, vine maple and waxy
green salal reclaim the soil.
Half-ripe berries survive
on tattered vines. Two finches
darted overhead, playing in the air.

## Saprophyte

I have walked often enough
through these thick wet autumn leaves
to have memorized the deep steps
and rich mulch pungent in my nostrils,
have learned somehow that decay
at the dead end of the year, in a sump of time,
is where a life, like a memory,
begins, first shoots creeping forth,
tiny gray beneath soaked earth.
No moon, no stars to rise above
bare black limbs and cumulus.

Down the valley through dense brush,
two coyotes in a thicket mourn
a moonless sky. Nighthawks
dive for moths. Mountain beaver
burrow deeper under heaped slash.
Hoe and ax lie idle in the shed.
An old coon scuttles along
down the hill through tangles of salal
and through a field of saplings.
Mushrooms. Saprophytes. Years
grind on, going nowhere.
In dead, decaying leaves,
we are finally reborn.

## Natural History

Late afternoon, autumn equinox,
and my daughter and I
are at the table, silently eating
fried eggs and muffins,
sharp cheese and yesterday's rice
warmed over.

We put our paper plates
in the wood-stove and go outside:
sunlight fills the alders with
the geometries of long blonde hair,
and twin ravens ride roller-coasters
of warm September air
out, toward Protection Island.

Together we enter the roughed-in room
beside our cabin and begin our chores together:
she, cutting and stapling insulation
while I cut and nail tight rows of cedar.

We work in a silence broken only
by occasional banter. I wipe the cobwebs
from nooks and sills, working on my knees
as if this prayer of labor could save me,
as though the itch of fiberglass and sawdust
were an answer to some old incessant question
I never dare remember.

When evening comes at last,
cooling arms and faces, we stop
and stand back to assess our work together.

And I remember the face of my father
as he climbed down a long wooden ladder
thirty years before. He was a tall strong sapling
smelling of tar and leather, his pate bald
and burnt to umber by a sun
blistering the desert.

He strode those rows of coops
with a red cocker spaniel and tousled boy-child
at his heel. I turn to look
at my daughter: her mop of blonde curls
catches the last trembling light of day.
Weary, her lean body sways.

Try as I might, I cannot remember
the wisdom of fourteen years, those pleasures
of discovery. Eron smiles. We wash up
at the wood-stove as the sun dies into
a candle-flame. A light breeze rustles the first yellow leaves
of autumn as boughs slowly darken.
A squirrel, enraged, castigates the dog
for some inscrutable intrusion,
and Eron climbs the ladder to her loft.

Suddenly, I am utterly alone,
a child gazing up at his father, a father
smiling down on his daughter.

A strange shudder comes over me
like a chill. Is this what there is
to remember: long days roofing coops,
the building of rooms on a cabin, the in-
significant meal?

Shadows of moments mean everything
and nothing, the dying landscapes
of remembered human faces frozen
in a moment. My room
was in the basement, was knotty pine,
back there in diamondback country.

The night swings out over the cold Pacific.
I pour a cup of coffee, heavy in my bones.
Soon, this fine young woman
will stare into the eyes of her own son or daughter,
years blown suddenly behind her.

Will she remember only this ache,
the immense satisfaction of this longing?
May she be happy, filled with the essential,
working in twilight, on her knees,
with her children, at autumn equinox,
gathering the stories of silence together,
preparing to greet the winter.

# A Cold Fire

An hour after sunset, Venus hangs
in the wintry mist of the west,
a cold fire burning alone above wet trees
and hills that fall and rise through fog.

We stand together a long time
hand in hand, watching
what we each have watched
a thousand times before.

Darkness and silence join hands
and spread over us the cool caress
of their breath. There is nothing
to say, nothing to do.

Startled into being something we'd
only dreamed of being,
we enter the exquisite abyss
of the first hour before heaven.

# Letter to John Logan from La Push

These heaped-up, half-paved streets
are no man's heaven, least of all
a drunk's. Stoked on wine
and brimming with regrets,
landlocked sailors swill their brew
below their rotting decks:
they dream tuna, money, and honey-haired girls
and fish from wreck to wreck.

You saw holy fog along this narrow beach
where, despite a sunless sky,
cedar timbers bleach.
You're more optimist, John, than I.

A drunk staggers sideways in the swell,
spitting blood, muscatel, and crabbing,
cursing his sunken hull. His Arctic breath
is icy on my cheek and in those native eyes
an ancient pain, like fog,
curls long and wide and dull.

# Lifer

*McNeil Island Correctional Center, 1:86*

Hunched over hard white bread
and plastic soup bowl filled with gruel,
he looked like a stork, a silly angel,
all neck and bony shoulder-wings
and awkward beak.

His head lifted, then fell
in a slow deliberate dance,
three, four times, doughy-skinned
in a gray room sickened by yellow light.
He kept his eyes shut tight.

Outside the prison dining hall,
a turnkey slammed and locked
the heavy iron gate. The old man placed
his palms together softly, raised
them to his stubbled chin,

crossed himself, and ate.

# Between You and Me

*Lemon Creek Correctional Facility, Juneau, Alaska*

The lonely man – who's been in prison – goes back
    to prison
each time he eats a piece of bread.
    – CESARE PAVESE

You believe another life will come,
the smell of the saloon, the bite
wind takes coming over the tundra.

Each bitter cup of coffee
steams alone. Is it dark? Sunrise
is Memory's other name.

Still, there will be an evening
when your hands unravel the slow
secrets of love, re-

learning that ancient form
of prayer. Behind you, the walls
will tremble with your shadows

till you glide through hazy air.
The bread you break, the soup
of hope, animals with nightfall

in their hair – these too
return in time. What the body
knows, it knows.

But nouns? Nouns
grind a man down:
*convict – prisoner – inmate.*

I too am just a man.
I understand the dignity of that.
I never bought

those names for wrong or right.
I will curb my taste
but not my appetite.

# Naming the Beast

There are no limits to masculine egotism
in ordinary life. In order to change the
conditions of life we must learn to see them
through the eyes of women.

— LEON TROTSKY

Woman, I return to you
first with my eyes
which are broken
by their cargo like wings
of a butterfly nailed
to a board under glass,

so beautiful and so useless –
I return to you
first with my eyes
which are bleeding.
Let others talk
about sleep, about dreams

and their meanings.
I dream a woman
in ice and mud, freezing,
begging me
to save her unborn baby,
the way I clawed

and clawed to reach her

until my nails were broken,
flesh ripped open
on splinters of ice
and the terrible
sound of her breathing.

I could not save her.
But there was no baby,
no woman, no ice.
It was only
a nightmare, you will say,
but it returns

and returns
like ordinary memory.
I return to you
with my eyes because
the terror is often
more bearable

for us that way,
because the huge
hole in your heart is
invisible, and no one
can see how even
the soul returns, weeping.

———

"Safe," they call it.
"A safe." That place

to protect you
from his rage. Ravaged eyes
peered down from the window
when I brought you,

and I knew they knew
that fear and pain. So they
locked you away like gold
that belongs to
no one but
yourself, you became

at last your own real
estate, a farm
and a temple
to which
only you
may hold title.

Thirty years of agony
are finally over,
your life reassembled. Call it
a dream if you will,
but the scars
are always real.

And now the stars
in your eyes
rekindle, little fires
of the soul burning

through the night
without heat,

refusing to go out,
lighting the far corners
of the deepest constellations
of your heart
with their glow:
you are alive.

And if I should cry, it is
only because the canary
sings more often
than the eagle, because
the butterfly, although
beautiful, is silent.

———

Battered, you said,
not beaten.
You took my hand.
Your voice was clogged
with grief. "Battered."
"Beaten."

There is a habit we have
of hearing
and not knowing
what we did not want

to know: a hum
of grief around us

like a boat droning
on the water, but
that moan is our own
suffering we could not name,
unspeakable agony
we could not name.

We are slowly
drowning
our own voices.
We are sinking.
You took my hand
and I wept.

I wept myself blind
in the street
when I saw you had
named the beast
and by naming,
defeated it.

Woman, I return
to you now
with my ears
which are full
of your tears
and your laughter:

neither victim
nor executioner,
call us simply
human,
naming what matters.

# Reading Seferis

*to Olga Broumas*

"Not many moonlit nights
have given me pleasure."
The stars spell out
the ancient mathematics
of the heart in huge
desolate zeros, ciphers
of nothing, and despite it all,
I care. There is a fatigue
in the crumbling of cities
for which there is no cure,
no penance or catharsis,
not even a prayer – only
the will to endure. The heavy
torpor of gray-brown air,
the lethargy of the soul –
by these we measure out
each crisis, each ancient debt
we don't repay the poor.

There are not many moons
I remember. The Sound
is blue where it reflects
the dark sky of night
or the bright sky of day.
*Amica silentia lunae,*
and each day the sun

drowns in fire and water,
a metaphor for nothing,
our unaccountable longing.
Some would call upon the moon
for power, for pure sexual
pleasure, but that is unholy
and denies both the sowing
and the reaping. The moon
is not a scythe that mows
the tall mute grass of heaven.

But we, Olga, are grasses
wavering in breezes
of politics and dollars, we
are the exiles of the earth,
the rooted and swarthy who see
the moon in everything
and think it a symbol
for our suffering. It is
the human mind that curves
into a razor, that harvests
human pain. We shall be
the chaff which flies
in the cutting, the lullaby
of fields that is not heard
on moonless nights because
only moonlight is romantic.

I hear the lullaby of victims
who are happy. Few are the moons
for them, and even these

are imagined. I imagine the
full moon of a smile, the moon
of my buttocks when I was a boy
and a prankster, the twin
moons of my lover's breasts,
the stars, oh, in her eyes
and I love her. Olga, these
are the maps, topographies
of the heart that tell us
everything: we are all
the victims; we are heroes
also, and slaves. Seferis says
heroes are the ones
move forward in the dark.

I remember the terrible
darkness of my childhood
and the fear. And the moon
was more fearsome, more awe-full
with its wails and howls
and its shadows. I remember
the moon as female, Loba, yesterday
when she raged. I tire so soon
of metaphor! I want to send you,
Olga, this alphabet of stars
which ask for nothing
and offer a little light
against the dark we wear;
I want to offer the warmth
of a lullaby, the kiss
of deep sleep, a reflection of the moon

reflected on the waters
of your song – so few

are the moonlit nights
that I've cared for.

# The End of the Road from Nantucket

This is the end of the whaleroad…

– ROBERT LOWELL

Dark. Dark. And dark winds
lash the rain into a frenzy.
The whole continent sleeps
its bloody sleep of history
with dreams of Sitting Bull
and Joaquin Murietta,
keelboats and outcasts
from this coast of no story
all the way back to the glory
of Nantucket. The Orcas
cry across the Sound, rise
through dark-swirled water,
and plunge again, and still
the unappeasable fears,
the hard rain and wind
of desperate sea-locked men
ride out the winter storm.

Dogfish slowly, slowly spin
beneath the waves. Friend, the
ancient gill-netter weeps
into this net he mends. No mystery
to his craft: a lull
can promise fortunes or get a
fisherman killed. What outlasts

this sea is praise: glory
slides into a sailor's eyes all hoary,
weatherworn and wry, a cause-
way for all the years. No Blighs,
no Ahabs survive to trouble water
along this coast. We will
ourselves no future: we steer
a course unmarked by dorsal fin
or blowhole that gives, again
and again each day, a style, a form.

Dark. Dark. And dark winds
swirl from the past. Wednesday
when we die, the sea will weep
no more, the lethal blistering
tides will rise into a full-
bodied swell lifting the last regatta
into doomsday, the masts
shattered like the Pequod's, forty
fathoms into Hell. For we
who have no past or cause,
the seas fill our eyes
with the hunger for slaughter,
a thirst for the manly thrill
of whaleblood, the sea's veneer,
of dying whales that win
no war, no time, no gain.
It's a human name we give the storm.

# Gnostology

Each return is a blessing,
a birthing. I come back again in the last light of evening
and the blue cups camas raises to catch the mist are
    dripping,
blackberries turning blue from green, and down
the narrow Strait of Juan de Fuca, foghorns
faintly sound.

I stand a long time outside, listening
to the dripping leaves and nighthawk cries.
Behind me, the dark house drips from the eaves.
I slide the wide door open
and breathe the stink
of stale beer and cigarettes
I smoked last week. The same books
clutter the table. The same poem dies
in the crude last unfinished line
I couldn't breathe.

I ease into my tattered chair in trembling light as
    the sunset
slides into a shadow
ghosting the dark Pacific.

Somewhere, the tide is
staggering over stones at
the feet of incoming swells;
the gulls are scavenging,

looping a last time over brine, searching for edibles
tangled in the wrack.

The moon slips between two cedars,
razor thin and curved into
a dazzling sliver of ice
simmering in the fog.
The dark of night settles in
on strong, steady feet.

This silence is not
profound – it's an old
friend, my beautiful dark daughter I haven't seen
in years, a longing, a soft
exquisite ache.

An hour flies. Another.
This life's
a summer reverie, a dream
flashing past unnoticed at the edge of sleep,
a simple gesture: a touch
or kiss of a friend.

Finally,
I rise
and step out of my clothes and stand on the porch
        in the mist,
suddenly naked,
lightly goose-fleshed,
more alive than I have been in days.

My whole body
responds to mist and air,
moist touch of evening bristling hairs of belly and legs,
    and I feel
my nipples' erection, my scrotum draw up against my
    groin,
my toes count every grain of earth beneath my feet.

Out in the empty night, thousands
and thousands of systems are at work –
lighting galaxies, whirling the billions
of years into a ball.

Are
the ants asleep inside
their catacombs of fir?
Are the chloroplasts resting their eyes?

With no prayer
on my breath, without hope or fear, without asking
what it is or what the seasons know,
I gather a long, slow breath,

breathe it,
kneel,
and bow.

# Requiem

*for Kenneth Rexroth*

I.

All day I wandered the difficult reverie of the sea
and the sea sang back to me that old song
of summer, "To Love is to Live," and the sun settled
lightly on the water. The interstellar silence between rainfall
and rainfall is all
that we need know of love, and all that we may learn of life
is that to die need not mean death.

The old hull slowly disintegrates among the stones
of its last long resting place and bears a silence
heavy like a shadow, iron railings flaking
off into rust, the old battered timbers nourishing salt air
and sea mist. But there was a time
she creaked with delight and bore tuna in her hold,
and strong young men worked her shifting decks.

Now that the nets are gone, brass fittings stripped
from the wheelhouse, cobwebbed and dank, now that
        the anchor
is dragged away? The tedious afternoons pass us by
unnoticed, the epics of our days. These tides
do not respect our work. And yet, to work
is the meaning of the tides and they steadily eat away
the memories of old labors we abandon.

Because it is summer and the sea is beautiful, we think it
enough just to be here, walking, sighing
beside the sea. There were others
who walked this beach to sing
a little song of charity and death.
They still sing, but far beyond
our ears. Few are they who hold in mind
our prehistoric life. Fewer still
learn to bow to what they cannot have.

Even in dry summer, the sea winds
sing our praise. But we
think it a cold song, shudder,
complain, and turn away.
Farther from home than we ever dreamed we could be,
the days break over us
like dreams these rains can't wash away.

If *to live* means *to love*,
to work gives form
to what we say: each day
we struggle to make the day.

There was a man, now gone, who sang this song to me.
I didn't believe it then. He begged
a price I didn't know how to pay. But now that he is gone,
*dead,* as they say,
I place my trust in him, in eighty years
of faith, his long life's love
that settles down like rain upon the sea, lightly down on
        everything,
like breath settles lightly into air.

II.

Suppose one human voice must speak,
suppose one human sound must stretch
across numberless gray casts of evening, in chill
of hoarfrost, before the puffs of hope
chimneys breathe against despair – then let
that voice be calming, a warming sound that bends
against the air curving back
across the breath it comes from, that no one hear
without the deliberate act of listening: our time
is near. The animal-like phrases
we attempt to trap in voices
move beyond our eyes, shadows
melting into shadows
we never learned to read.

When a man ascends the stage of his own imagining,
he delivers there the grand summation
of his suffering, his one long
accounting of his days which disappeared
more quickly than his faith. His song
is plain. His music,
lowly, like his shame. The stillness in the air
at eventide, the stillness in the leaves at that
singular moment
before they ride the last ride down to earth,
the still perfectly still body of the hunter with his finger
        on the trigger,
squeezing lightly between the hammers of his heart:
these motionless moments
we only glimpse in passing.

After love, after the soft white cry of love
is stoppered in the throat,
these little revolutions of the soul are caught
between breath and breath, between the blood
and the body in its tremors. Who then
will remember the ambiguity of desire, duplicity
hidden in the semi-public kiss? Per-
functory and self-serving. Wavering, …
hesitant, … faulty, … no wonder
we strangle on our doubts. Raccoons that haunt
        these shores
blend into the dusk. Can we
do less? We see them
walk on tiny hands to steal scraps we leave.

It is only when we must move, similarly simply,
toward that secret something
basic as our breathing that we
can learn to trust. What troubles us
most deeply is ourselves – a voice that longs to make
itself into a fist or a hand
to touch. We want to slow our pace
to match the little steps of animals who feed at night.
If we must blend into the blending grays
of dusk, then we must learn
to wait, watching from the corners of our eyes
until the remembered glimpse of warming fires
blazes up again
a long way down the coast around the bend
where evening fog comes toward us hushed and slowly
like a friend.

III.

Out the long road with its ruts and cracks
and tire-battering patches, past fields
of spotted cows and fat summer horses, past
the last few stands of woods, past new houses
with indoor plumbing and interest rates,
out,
past the end of the city water line and up
the hill beyond the old shake mill into
a world of promise,

and then the dirt country road
lined with alder and evergreen, broad leaf
fern, rhododendron, camas
and camomile, and up
the narrow drive
where branches batter my battered truck,

I wheeze
to a stop. This brief northwestern summer allows
a little dust
to remind me
of all those summers back

in that country I'll never shake
from my boots: red dust
and prickly heat. Now scraggle of underbrush
almost too thick to walk through,
but I walk out,
climbing through it, smelling it,
watching for juncos and swallows and thrushes,

boots growing damp from night-mist,
senses confused with the memory of mountains:
    Wasatch,
Rockies, Tetons, Sangre de Cristos, Brooks Range,
Chugach, and now, suddenly,

the Olympics, immensely blue
in the distance. And I know
how the rain never stops in Ketchikan,
how the rain never came
to Utah,…

all those countries now
one country in
my mind.…
so different, so lonely
that poetry can't reach it. Nor can I.

But I wade through it, tangle
and bramble, I wade and plunge
through rotting broken limbs and twigs toward
bluffs rising over the Sound where winds
grow thick with salt-smells
and islands in the distance
rise, rise and fall
in swells: San Juans, Queen Charlottes
of Canada; and beyond them,
across the long Pacific Rim,
Japan
and northern China.

I would speak across years. T'ao Ch'ien,
do you hear?

And why is it
I must come out here alone? Never with
a friend. For a man, for a man
in the middle of his years, there is a need
without name, an old memory or promise
broken: my mother, almost eighty now, but years
and years ago, my mother,
her eyes a river of tears
for something I'd said
for no reason.

Gull-cries.
Cormorant scuds.
Clouds and clouds and clouds.
My father four years dead
and buried in that half-imagined land. He died
holding his woman's hand. I learn to live
alone
in a house I slowly build and know
my own daughter will likewise
wound me one day.

My brown Persephone so far away,
listen to this sea: it churns, it breaks against these black
basaltic bluffs, and in the blue
swirl and curl of water, tentacles
of kelp beds absently waver.

Suppose I cried out against
the immensity of these blues – *ocean, sky,*
or *mountain?*
Would anyone hear
or care? I wouldn't give a damn. When the sun
begins its plunge, it makes me
sickly dizzy – birds, suns, sea-wrack.
I'd paint these mountains black. Little wonder
old Jeffers grew so vile: he knew
what we feel inside.

Thirty years ago, I used to lie
on my back in the haystack to listen to the stars.
Dusk then was a kind of silence I haven't heard since,
the unutterable gray
dying light across a range of gutted mountains
smoky-black with greed.

Lie quiet.
Listen. Is that
the first nighthawk
searching yellow evening light? The sound
of evening appetites:
*peee-ik, peee-ik, peee-ik.*

Turning to the trail back home, there is
so much vanishing behind us, so very much
to come, and all that goddamned country
spread out
beyond all comprehension,
beyond imagination.
Pray that it will heal.

Coming across me here,
along these old logging trails,
along game trails leading us back from the sea,
do you think me a gentle man, but sad? – not unlike
that man you knew once as a child,
who wagered with the sun
and lost,
who made you lovely promises – so long ago
that you can't quite remember,

although you remembered for a time. This sea, you
     think,
smells like the great salt wastelands of
the West. The same gulls break and cry. The same hearts
break night after night
when the same voices
steal into our sleep.

Kochininako, Yellow Woman,
take my hand.
This silence that steals into my speech
is there because
there are so many promises
I've tried and tried to keep.

IV.
Is it still there, Canyon de Chelly,
high walls streaked
the color of new blood or of fire?

Once – a long time ago, it is true – but once
I went there alone, looking

for god-knows-what, and found
what the Greeks called *Eikos*, a holy place,

evening sunlight orange,
fiery as all history, and I walked for a time
in no particular direction, lost
to all purpose, but
learning,
slowly learning: apple trees, pear trees,
a spotted pony in a narrow corral.

I was a child of no country
but the country of the heart. I felt
the hands of the dead slide up
beneath my shirt.
And now, when I write or speak,
there is dying on my hands, dying
to flavor my speech.

I tried to sleep. A quarter-moon
slipped over the canyon rim
to filter through the trees. The flanks of the canyon
were fleshy in a light
as after twilight
when I rose from a brown saddle blanket
to walk among the ghosts: my body
moved as though it belonged
to another, an ancient melancholy
dragging me down into the past.

But every canyon, like every street,

is a doorway, we are beggars
knocking softly for entry. The busy people
pass us by in silence, their eyes focused carefully
an inch beyond our heads or
just beyond our feet. For fear,
they look away.
Our secret whispered entreaties
are fruitless, falling
like dry grass through summer drought,
and we turn again
toward night and thirst of heat.

Did I sleep? I remembered the body
of a woman I loved once, who
wouldn't speak, how, with her child
nursing, her breasts dried up, and nothing, she said,
would ever be the same. Her furtive eyes
glistened in the dark like little fires
burning a hill, and I held her face
for nothing in my hands until
I thought it would break.

Sweet, delicious smell of rain.

So many years since the hoeing. It is too easy
saying, Here is Ira Hayes
dying in a ditch. My people were not heroes,
but died there, too. No one mourned
except when the crop was good.

The waters and the beggars come and go,

the cruel light of years claws our eyes.
Are there still memories in the ashes
rains wash slowly from the canyon? The memory
of women weaving baskets
from a time before they were meant for tourists?
Is anguish the only sound of water? Or is it
longing? And what would it mean
if we could walk again together
through ruins years have left behind, our hands
    together,
eyes steady on each other's eyes? Would
the same crickets sing down there along the river
if we paused for love on the bank?

I who inhabit
the River-with-one-bank
have been too long with the sea, too long
with the slow rub of fog
and all those old songs
of the dying.

When light rain comes calling,
when it kisses the edge of my sleep, I dream
of scarlet ocotillo flowers
blooming after rain,
so long in the waiting, in the desert, waiting,
their blossoms so suddenly, *ocotl,*
torches, burning after rain. Whether their burning
is the burning of cities, the remembrance of Canyon
    de Chelly
when armies passed in the night to torch

houses, fields, and orchards,
when the dogs and children died, –

or whether it might be
my own heart,
our hearts, inflamed
by some spark without reason –
that old hope and joy –
I cannot say.

v.

The dead of summer and nothing moves,
not the sky of weathered slate
nor the faces of strangers
pasted in their rooms above the street,
expressionless or strained. The joyous intervals
we pass by
remain mute, committed now
to memory's coldest cells.

*Once,*
the poet sang, *once only.* And then no more?
The murky tide that washed our feet
draws slowly back to sea.
The young couple in the doorway
linger to embrace.
This, and then the earth?

Yesterday was berries on the beach.
I dozed beside a fire and heard
or dreamed foghorns on a summer afternoon

like sirens enticing us
toward reefs hidden by the waves.
I woke, chilly and afraid.

This dead weight we carry
like an ancient grief is ours
because we will it – the lonely burden
of the verb *to be*
as it becomes attached
to *living* or *alive*, day by day. So it's not to say

we can't, or won't, go on.
But on this earth, in
the middle of our trespass, we are
invisible, we are only shadows
sliding into night, pausing to give names
to things that shape our passing: *saguaro,*
*thimble-berry, madrone.* Or *charity.*
Or *love.*

Tell me it isn't fruitless, this moment
in which John Coltrane breaks
my heart from a phonograph, or that moment
long ago when I was lost in
Beethoven's great Pastoral as the wind
swept away the desert endlessly.

As long as the tongue can open to the vowel,
as long as we can rise into
each day, just once, rise, and, rising,
move the hand

to *act*, it remains for us to praise:
the fine red dust of Escalante,
light rain or mist of summer on the northwest coast,
almond groves of the northern San Joaquin,
the clarity of temple bells, Kyoto after rain.

Could I feel the fingers that brushed my lips
just once,
so very long ago, then
I could praise.

*Good-bye,* we say, meaning
*happy passing,*
or *kind beyond.* But we
are only shadows
pausing as we pass high over the earth to say
our little praise. The old madrone
that trembles in the wind
can't help us, the absolute calm of animal eyes at night
cannot be our calm.

But once, once
leaning in a door
that opens the other world,
we pass our moment,
and suddenly know the earth
that we were a part of, once.

II.

## The Cartographer's Wedding

Nobody knows what love is anymore –
not the groom in his rental suit
flushed with desire, not the bride
blushing in her one-day dress and flowers
smoldering with the fires of expectation.
Nobody knows, and I least of all.

Still, we are here, against all reason,
the products of that ancient spoken
or unspoken vow. To the east, across
nearly insurmountable summits caked
with snow, the Great Plains rise
and fall while we continue to remain

steady as November rain, having grown
accustomed to a cold that never freezes,
to a shade of deep, spectacular green
intact, season after season. And so we find
ourselves outside in fog, in hoarfrost,
in rain or snow, living as we do

at the edge of a continent or a dream,
living perhaps with our hearts
not in our hands, but on our lips,
although they are seldom spoken.
(Friendship hereabouts is assumed –
like an old mackinaw or a blanket.)

But that times comes, and it *will* come,
when you try to recite the names
or find the odd, almost familiar faces
that move beyond the old events, like fog,
that made you what you are. Years
that disappeared like falling stars

are lovely to remember. And there will
be time a-plenty for flowers on a grave.
No, nobody knows what love is. Nobody
understands the past. Saddled with
all the hopes that will outlast
a lifetime's dedication, we, –

groom, bride, friend and friend –
we step into the day amazed to find our-
selves among companions eager to weather
the winds of change which turn us
heavenward, poor fools together,
never to learn what love is, we

who map the country where it lives.

# The Journey

the heart / never fits / the journey
– JACK GILBERT

To begin, it begins
and ends with the heart, that long
tunnel with darkness
at its end. So that the journey is a kind
of defeat the ordinary heart survives.

Like the man who buys flowers for his love:
of course, the flowers die. He dies.
Or she dies. Or is it their love?
Such a sequence of events we name The Journey
and which, that it might live, the heart contrives.

# Homage to Trakl

> The dead have their own tasks.
>
> – RILKE

## I. DE PROFUNDIS

Black rain in a stubbled field,
the lone brown tree, and a whisper
of wind to haunt the empty houses.

It is beautiful to walk alone
in the final silence of the light,
to gather the growing dark into our arms
as we go, to embrace its thistles.

Far from the villages, we can hear insects call,
tides riding the distances, and evening animals
the mind supplies. I could tell you how skies
turn to stars, how stars first throb and then tremble,
but you have seen the night.

I saw the good light die
upon your tongue and found myself on a moor,
lost among rubble and waste and strange sounds
without names, stiff with cold, terrified and beguiled
by the song dead angels sing to the wild.

You are gone into our blood and dusty stars
tremble softly in the mire.

## ii. Helian

In its loneliest hours, the spirit
loves a walk in the sun between
the yellow walls of summer.

Long evenings I wasted on wine,
chatter, the sweet sonata of laughter,
and the absolute still of night:
these were the seeds of my planting.

I wandered the black labyrinth
of November bowing my head
beneath decaying limbs where thrushes
sang alone in the dark.

If I glimpsed the mad son, the deranged
sweat of his sleep, his weeping –
no one saw him except it was night.

The dead are resurrected just at dusk
when the nameless goddess gapes, swallows light,
and closes those blue, bottomless eyes.

## iii. Lament at Grodek

Twin eagles, Sleep and Death,
circle his head all night.
The icy wave lifts up
his bruise-blue body
and shatters it on the reef.

The sea sings its lament,
and the sisters of the sea
grow quiet, silent stars hesitate
and die out,
all the weapons fail.

Wrapped in the skirts of night,
his mouth broken, he bleeds
a long road leading into questions
only autumn answers.
Soon, he will burst into flame, soon

his song will harden into bronze,
and fall back over us,
and crush us,
and burn us black with shame.

IV. To One Who Died Young

My dark angel, my demented one,
you must have been a child
at one time, you must have descended
those stone steps in autumn in Monchsberg
smiling strangely. Could you hear

what the stones were singing? Could you
hear the deer's lament? What purple sun
died in bare branches of the elm?
What flower turned to blood
as it blossomed on your tongue?

The evening bells were always blue
like this. The stars are always good.
You would have loved these stars tonight,
you would have walked alone and silent
under dead elms lining the riverbank.

# The Body of Summer

I.
After hours of small talk and music,
after the coffee and conversation,
I part your knees
to kiss you:
your whole body buzzes
like a field of bees
and I savor
the summer's honey.

II.
You wake me at dawn,
warm breasts pressed against
my thighs, your breath warm
and lingering:
far to the south,
in forests dripping rain,
temple bells are ringing.

# A Rose for Solitude

I.

A man wades the deep north,
bending into the day. Birch trees are black
against falling snow
whole mountains vanish in.

The flakes are wet and heavy with spring.
Already Cook Inlet begins to break up, huge chunks
of ice thrust up, pools warmed by last week's sun
collecting into currents. This sudden city
is gray against gray skies.

II.

If only we could touch
the things of this world
at their center, if we could only hear
tiny leaves of birch
struggling toward April,
then we would know.

But we walk on through falling snow
just as before, through mile after mile
of deep snow, through mountains and valleys of it,
more snow falling in huge wet flakes,
no two quite alike.

III.

The old poet in his seventieth year
wrote: "Change rules the world. / And man

but a little while." The moon tonight will be full.
It is March of the year
forty-thousand eighty-two
on the secular calendar.

The old poet whom I love
is dying. And I
am suddenly in the middle of my life.

IV.
In the fortieth dawn of my journey.
Turning toward my fortieth year, I turn toward home.
     The path
I follow vanishes before my eyes:

No road shows the way,
Kotaro said in a poem, the road
follows behind.

When Su Tung-p'o was
an old old man, his house burned down.
He laughed, "Now I can see the stars!"

This world is only process, a single
monumental motion
without beginning, without end.

We like to think this world is ours,
but we belong to it,
to a world just being born.

v.

Creak of soft snow. My breaths go out in little puffs
only to disappear. From far off, I faintly hear
the rattle and clatter of a train.

No wind.
The ravens hop first on this foot,
then on that, around a scrap of bread.

Watching their dance, I suddenly feel,
for no reason, the small coal
of my heart flicker, then grow.

vi.

The mystics say
now that the planets align,
there will be great change.

Some predict gloom.
Some, glory.

Planets are nothing to me.
I say, It is snowing.

vii.

And if, as I pass,
I should look you in the eye,
do not be afraid: I want
only to glimpse the emptiness
at the center of your heart,
I want to reach for you

because I know,
as you do,
we might never have met.

VIII.
"Life after life after life
goes by," the poet said.
And how many lives go by us every day
and never quite touch the earth?
And how many bodies shamed
by sudden light?

Gray birds circle and twine through trees.
They have no cry.
Each moment is
everything we have. And more
than we can use.

IX.
Yesterday, in a colder climate,
alone in a frozen city,
a pilgrim climbed frozen streets toward home.

Winds scorched his face, his parka zipped tight,
hood drawn close against chill.

Inside his shirt, clutched against his heart,
he held a single long-stemmed rose, the little bud
warmed by whatever warmth he had.

It was just a little flower
for nothing in this world.

Its thorns beaded his skin
with blood, red bud
nestled to his nipple.

Somehow, he carried it home
to bloom in dead winter.

x.
Others wade the deep north.
Others will pass by
in reverence for whatever this country knows.

Another may offer a rose
against this solitude, a hopeful breath, a hand
to hold back the night.

Summer flies.
And then the snows return.
We may one day be strangers again.

## Pastoral

Can you still stand out on that balcony
and see far off across the tops
of stunted birch trembling in spring winds,
dirty inlet piled high with snow
and ice, can you still hear the drone
of planes, the whine of single engines
curving over hills and houses
above those filthy streets? I see you
staring through the empty afternoon
at nothing,
waiting perhaps for some simple thing
that never comes, some gesture from the land.

Dark red wine nourished me
like soil when I explored
secret depths of tangled brush,
soft blue pools of water, roses
still hidden deep within their buds.
I, too, am hovering – a hummingbird,
a bee. Everything's like that: an old song
sung slightly out of key, a memory
of a gentle pastorale someone played once
perfectly. I, too, watch, but cannot see.
Listen for the land to have its say,
for the music of what may be.

# George Seferis in Sonora

> It is most true that eyes are form'd to serve
> The inward light, ...
>
> – SYDNEY, "ASTROPHEL AND STELLA"

No, I can't touch these mountains.
I have no word for the long shadows of saguaros
lengthened by the full moon of April. I've seen
how you wrap these mountains in highways, how
the natural numbers of Sonora accumulate
until you suddenly realize
they always total zero. At 4 a.m.
when the traffic dies and the moon embraces the Pacific,
I'm up
and drinking coffee, my nose in George Seferis.
Whatever you told me, I had to learn it by ear,
I had to memorize the touch – I couldn't believe my eyes.

How else to account for fingers that touched me once
and then vanished: of course they were roses
dying of the sun, they were songs doves sang
to begin another morning. It's always that
exactly: the untouchable other world
that touches us most deeply. Paris lay down
with a shadow, he lay down with an empty tunic,
and thousands died, but they did not die
for Helen. It was no goddess or mortal
they died for: not Helen, but the idea of Helen betrayed
    them.

And surely this desert is a woman who knows

God first invented blood
and then the thirst for blood, that each man is a Paris
who returns, anonymous, clutching an empty tunic.
To speak of the desert, I must return
to the Ancients, to the memory of some unspeakable
  failure.

Even to speak of Troy
in this city in Sonora, even to dream of Troy –
it is brutal. So I rise, old somnophobiac, before the day
  begins,
to write in the blood of our race, to save
what cannot possibly be saved,
and now, the first songbirds long before dawn,
  mockingbirds,
add their *gloriae, gloriae*, to the morning.

———

Sometimes the dove, that old cliché,
is more a moan than a song
when it sings *woe, woe*, and huddles on its limb.
A veil of fragile clouds
marbles the eastern sky. In Alexandria, they say,
it's the nightingale who wounds us. Here, we listen
to the terrible silence of the past, the enormous cost
of our decision to forget. Yesterday, as you trimmed
a dying bougainvillea, you pointed
across the way to another, entirely in blossom.

"They like the sun," you said, "and this one
gets very little." Oh, it was the color of blood,
it was beautiful all right.


And I wanted to give you a flower, but the garden
was all weeds, there were no roses, no asphodels
for me to bring to ease our mutual regret,
only these few coarse words
an old man sings in a broken voice when he's humbled
by a desert. There's a desert
each of us endures. It's beautiful there,
and deadly: whatever we give away
comes back to us, it's true, so I bring you
the whole of the moon as it passes, the fallen
petals of roses crushed into a powder,


this sort-of-a-song
rattling my heart with its singing.


But it's not about a desert. No,
I can't reach your mountains, I have no word
for these highways wrapping a heart for storage.
When the moon returns
bulging with its promises and warnings,
I will have no word to name them.


The roads that lead back from Sonora as though from
    the ancient temple
are a song a choir sings
in a long-forgotten language, the long body of our
    dreaming,

a lattice-work for rose-vines blooming by inward light
our eyes were made for seeing. And now,
in the harsh first light of day,
mockingbirds sing *gloriae, gloriae absurdus.*

# A Word for Spring

We've returned; we always set out to return
to solitude, a fistful of earth, to the empty hands.

    – GEORGE SEFERIS, "A WORD FOR SPRING"

Once more we step
from the cold solitudes of winter
into the solitudes of spring. Once more,
yellow daffodils and lilies
are the cruelest month.
I used to love to walk down Water Street
where crates of oranges and bananas
and heads of cabbage and lettuce were
stacked shoulder high. I used
to watch the unknown people pass
beside the miracle of the sea
talking to each other
as though the sea were a thousand miles
away and didn't know the secrets of our blood.

Sometimes, I think the sea is
listening to our lies; sometimes,
I think it hears us groping in the dusk.
If it does, it remains at ease
despite us. If we could understand
the rhythms of the tides, if we
could reach into the shadows of the bay,
we too could sleep through the long
and lengthening sunshine of the day.

We pause between the coffee and the cigarette,
between the talk that wakes us and the sleep
of solitude that punctuates our speech,
studying our hands like exiles
bent above a map that set us on our way.

The secret meeting place
where water and land join hands
could be our place. Were it not
for the red and the white of our veins,
our hearts would pump
pure sea water to our minds and lungs
and we would learn to breathe
according to the moon. But we
are lonelier than that. Someday soon,
the old days will come back. I loved
the bread I broke between my hands,
the taste of wine from someone's lips,
the emptiness of Water Street at night when spring
was ripe and everything was mine.

## Black Marsh Eclogue

Although it is midsummer, the great blue heron
holds darkest winter in his hunched shoulders,
those blue-turning-gray clouds
rising over him like a storm from the Pacific.

He stands in the black marsh
more monument than bird, a wizened prophet
returned from a vanished mythology.
He watches the hearts of things

and does not move or speak. But when
at last he flies, his great wings
cover the darkening sky, and slowly,
as though praying, he lifts, almost motionless,

as he pushes the world away.

## Kah Tai Purgatorio

I could carry a little boat out
through sandy hillocks and marsh grass
and slip it into the water and slide
over that blue-green glass in silence.

I could cruise the waterways of winds
around this small lagoon where
terns nestle into shadows and herons wade.
I could, I could.

I want, like the little body of water,
to let my body reflect the stars and moons
of midnight. I want to lie that still.
I've seen this water calm as a dreamy boy.

But then I'd have to, sooner or later,
return. And doing so, I'd have to choose.
And any bank I chose
would be the world.

# Nihil Obstat

Bees are building stairways toward heaven.
Soon, the world will cloud over and bees
fall silent and die among dead blossoms
of scotch broom and thistle.
We who often buzz
among our own works will not listen. This
is called natural history and is left
for specialists to explain. Someday everything
will be explained in footnotes of basalt
and granite, in igneous thumbprints
of another century.

For now, there is the song
September sings to welcome autumn.
We cannot save the bees. We cannot save
one another.
Birds of prey
staggering down the skies will wait for us
at the other end of history,
as we, stung
by the brevity of their song, enter
the resonant long corridor of dying light
that leads us not toward heaven, but toward home.

## October Frost

The poor cricket longs for a song, and I
know it, I can feel it in the air
at dusk when shadows grow and October frost
settles all the dust.

Between us on this table,
a bottle of warm red wine, the pen,
the ashtray, and the wood. Soon enough,
the dark will nail us down. Our hands
hold a cup, a knife, a noose.

Even for a cricket,
song may mean no more than an act
of contrition, unreasonable fear of the dark,
or its own expression of this alien life
on a fertile, fading planet.

Whatever
we lose or have lost, we find it
everywhere, in someone else's hands, and we know
that something's wrong that has no name
of its own.

The poor, poor cricket
wants to sing. The dust begins to freeze.
In some other country, in some other time,
he might mean something, he might be important
enough to cage.

But it is the end of the day
at the end of October when the year begins
to close. In the wine cup, in the pen or the air,
we can feel it, in our bones: we don't belong.

The poor poet wants a dithyramb.
The cricket longs for a song.

# Passport

When you get there, it will be the same life
you dreamed about in youth:
the tall, narrow, unwashed window
at the far end of a musty room;
a small table with the open book;
the chair, just as before.

Outside in the streets
there are fish for sale; and strange cloth
from seaports; beggars and disease.
The alleys vibrate in the heat.
The wine is warm and red
and thick in the afternoon.

And you walk out toward evening
past the cemetery on the hill,
then turn and come back into your room
and light the evening candle.

# Kali

When at last you came down from your hills
to walk this sacred valley,
you were shocked
to find it ruined, fields bare,
its fig groves burned, its temple
a disaster.

The air has turned volcanic.
The shadows grow shadows where
something almost feline moves – a wolf
or a bear.
Under a choir of stars,
you strain to hear.

No sound.
The cross-hatched light
falls like shattered monuments.
Once, when the sea was still sweet,
you dreamed you could touch the Goddess,
you set out on your journey.

You have come in search of Her temple
and found Her common door.

# Elegy

Always, the world we invent or build
around us remains dark. But there is always
a door or window, and, beyond it, light.

We cannot know what moves out there
in the night – a dog, a horse, an animal
that we can't name.

All around us shadows deepen
and we sink into ourselves
afraid.

Everything we see we perceive
as an extension of ourselves and that
is why we question

the intentions of anything that breathes.
The cold grows steadily in the dark.
As the hours breed, we reach

but cannot touch the animals
that move more quickly than our need.
And so it comes to pass

that we can only watch dark shapes
grow darker with the light,
their wide unblinking eyes

blazing with fire and ice.

## Hermes Rising

In the middle of the night you have opened your eyes
and risen.

And walked out naked into the night where the world
is suddenly still and the cities
have been swallowed whole and everything's present
as never before:

the air rising around you like waves,
shadows falling off, trees sinking
farther and farther into the earth
which smells of passion.

You dreamed you were chained to a cliff,
a phoenix

gnawing at your liver, you dreamed you were
falling and falling,

but now you know that you can't fall.
And you breathe in the light of stars –
Sirius brightest of all – and your flesh takes in
that light, and you listen

for the sound of feathers,
for the slow thrum of your blood that never lies,

and you lift up your arms to the night,
certain you can fly.

## Sheep to Slaughter

Like a sacred cow on the Ganges,
I feel the years turn to meat and metaphysics.
I cannot understand. I look out at the world
and everything I see slides by
in a haze, or I go down on my knees
for prayer or sleep and shadows rise up
like icons. You, too,
chew on the same old questions –
our classical cud and useless benedictions.
Tender and unaccountable.
The untouchable touches us.
What is beautiful alters.

# Animus Mundi

My world would not fit into yours.
And you would never enter mine.
Safe behind your deadbolt locks,
you are lighting the evening lamps,
turning pages in the latest Book of the Dead,
wondering perhaps if your name is among them,
among the pseudonyms of angels
or among the names of ash.

Did you think I knew the way?
Did you think you saw my shadow
moving among shadows in the rubble
of the devastated city?
The night lies down at last
beside the mountain. The voice you hear
is memory, that tattered rag
of glory.

When you call out to me,
your voice hangs in the smoke
above the burning river
where birds fall quiet
and desire rusts
and everything you trusted runs away.
I could not fit into your world, nor lay aside
my doubts. I'll marry the darkening dust.

## Seated Figure

It is a long way from there to here.
It is longer than all the old roads of exile,
longer even than the silence of the heron.
The landscapes changed. Someone
numbered the dead, someone mapped the pain.

Once, they say, the animals came to us,
and licked our palms for the salt,
and looked at us with huge, knowing eyes,
then turned and left
alone. And entered Paradise.

# Dresden Cattle

Oh, the ruins of the human heart.
Like a barn gone up in flames,
like a bombed cathedral,

the shadows of almost human forms
fall or rise or slide
silently by, entering the dark

and light by turns – Napoleon
or the Slavs that died
along the dying Elbe.

The old blue marbled hands
of the mason set stone upon stone,
and the bloody hands of the bitter

made them shatter.
We were herded through the streets
like cattle. We cried

but no one came. It is one thing
to love another human being,
another to know

and remember
the way the beautiful died.

# Treblinka Lights

The clatter of hooves on cobblestone:
everything stops together.

In Treblinka, the snow has stopped falling,
and the inmates
lie in their racks.

Some are punished for reading,
some who witnessed crimes
have turned their backs
and listen for the footsteps
of Thanatos in the night.

The ants are stacking the cold.
Some one moves a hand.
Someone moves a heart.

It is spring in the old country.
There is neither hope nor light.

One dreams, one dies,
one remembers a child
while one is turning to ice.
Thanatos makes us equal in his eyes.

## Cloistered

It was summer on the north coast,
the wrong coast they call it in the East.
It was summer. And summer means rain.

Rain dissolved islands in the Sound,
it buried mountains and turned the ocean gray.
I listened to it rattle at my window.

Funny, how you wake some days
in the middle of the morning and know
somehow a part of the world has died,

another language lifted from our tongues,
another way of knowing. And you don't know
whether the pulse you feel is yours

or is the fading beat of the world.
An eagle is not a symbol for a thing.
It was early summer or late spring,

I listened to the rain. For all
its tenderness and wealth, the earth
is often a meagre gift.

But to know and not to speak
is the greatest grief. Listen.
The world flows away like a wave.

## Hellenic Triptych

Forehead on forearm, eyes unfocused,
he listens to rain pelting wet earth that smells
of dreams and destinations, of departures which
preceded no arrival. Alone with the long afternoon,
he longed for starlight through windows,
for the soft, hollow breath of the sea as it sounds
through the broken conch of the human voice
traveling its distance alone.

There was a time he thought of his body
as a temple for Helen, a time when the twin fires of his
     tongue
were his daughters, Justice and Mercy, but
that is the way of the young. Helen,
kidnapped by Theseus much as our bodies are taken:
for the moment – before the life escapes into Hades –
and we waken to dawn confused, everything forgotten,
everything but Helen.

And so he sets sail from Troy, forehead
bent to forearm, the afternoon slipping by
with its cargo of dream and remembrance.
So that is how the summer died.

———

At dawn, he'd taken
a solitary step and entered

the nearly perfect syntax of the world.

It would be simple to die for a Helen.
It would be easy to set sail, to turn one's back on the ruins,
to acquire the grammar of wisdom
at the small cost
of some small life:
to perfect a civilization.

Arrival is not destination, nor death
a suitable answer.

Each step the first step; each step the final:
each road a crossroad: each tree
articulates a tree. – It is that which comes closest
but passes, that suggestion of perfection,
that makes the flesh its home.

————

And now, he knows, the evening comes
with its torment and its thugs
demanding taxes. And then the anonymous night
with its quicklime of desire,
its starlight and retribution.

That is how this window came to look out
of grief, on the charred monuments of Troy:
it would be good to give one's life for the beautiful
if the beautiful would last. But the world
casts us out and it is impossible to touch anything

except one another. So we reach out when we can

for the outstretched hand of another
knowing that when it is withdrawn...

Head tilted forward
almost as though to pray, he buries

his eyes in his forearm.
And the gesture
is almost perfect.

III.

## "True Illumination is Habitude"

A perfect half-moon glistens
in the mist high over
the young bamboo.

The smoke-stained glass
I watch it through
makes a perfect halo

around it, as though
the moon were full. Below,
the trees are doubly dark

where no breeze lifts
a leaf – nothing moves
that doesn't move

toward sleep. You move,
in another room,
into the Dreamtime world,

your hair flooding out
in soft waves
around your face.

The night is so
perfectly still
I can hear your every breath

above my beating heart.
The fire's long since
gone out.

Alone by my lamp,
I read Rexroth's
*Signature of All Things*,

and once again,
like that swift bird
rising from its ashes,

the old ghost rises
from the wreckage of
this world

to touch my semi-
conscious life.
Poetry, Tu Fu says,

that will last
a thousand generations
comes only as

an unappreciated life
is passed.
I lay aside the book

and rub my weary eyes
just as Po Chu-i did
reading Yuan Chen

on his boat, by candlelight
a thousand years ago.
I sit motionless

in the motionless night
while mist
deepens

and the whole house
cools,
and I listen to your breath

and measure it against
this slow, insistent tolling
of our flesh.

## Scrutability

Tu Fu, old and ravaged by consumption,
bent over his mulberry paper and wrote
the characters "single" and "wild goose,"
his eyes weakened by the moonlight.

Because it was October in his life,
he refilled his cup with wine.
His joys were neither large nor many.
But they were precise.

## At Rexroth's Grave

Off the bluff, huge white sails wind
among oil rigs pumping the Pacific.

Every grave but Rexroth's
faces toward the sea.

He faces the continent
alone, an old explorer,

hawk-eyed, sharp-tongued,
walking inland with his oar.

# A Dragon in the Clouds

It is solstice, –
hot, dry,
air too heavy to move,
mountains hazy blue.

I have been baking in the sun
with Euripedes' fable of Helen.

And now, quietly,
a finch has flown down from the cedar
to perch on the windowsill.

And I realize
she is curious,
she is watching,

and has cautiously stepped closer.

The beauty of the tragic,
the tragedy of the lovely,

she doesn't know or care to remember.

She knows two things:
the world is flat,
and that she lives

on this side

of the only river
she cannot fly across.

She looks at emeralds
in the grass and sees
only common seed.

And now she has come closer
once again, head cocked,
surveying my naked body.

Her eyes are large
and wearied by their knowledge,

like Kawabata's eyes
which knew
only sadness and beauty.

I close my book very slowly,
lay my head on my arms,
and look her in the eye:

she has become my lover
and my dharma master.

Morris Graves says birds
inhabit a world without karma.

# Tammuz in the Garden

Stretched naked in the sunlit garden,
how can I not name the flowers
blooming one by one,

how can I not think of lovely Helen
when she was still a goddess,
kidnapped as she picked

from a small garden such as this
a small bouquet, her loveliness,
her innocence

taken by violence and lust.
But the garden does not judge.
It rises in its season

as evidence of being –
the soil in the hand is the flesh
becoming –

the garden blooming is the brief
declarative sentence,
seed syllable

from the heart of great silence.

## The Gift of Tongues

Everything I steal, I give away.
Once, in pines almost as tall as these,
same crescent moon sliding gently by,
I sat curled on my knees, smoking with a friend,
sipping tea, swapping Coyote tales and lies.

He said something to me
about words, that each is a name,
and that every name is God's. I who have
no god sat in the vast emptiness silent
as I could be. *A way that can be named*

*is not the way.* Each word reflects
the Spirit which can't be named. Each word
a gift, its value in exact proportion
to the spirit in which it is given.
Thus spoken, these words I give

by way of Lao Tzu's old Chinese, stolen
by a humble thief twenty-five centuries later.
The Word is only evidence of the real:
in the Hopi tongue, there is no whale;
and, in American English, no Fourth World.

# Getting It Wrong Again

"...civilizations are as short-lived as
days of our lives...."

— CZESŁAW MIŁOSZ

and slowly, in the middle, I close the book and lay aside
the unreal world.

Clouds continue to gather overhead, outside,
sliding in from the sea.

Nothing distinguishes them, one from the other,
but bulk or weight or the pathetic tint
gray sunlight lends their hair.

Thus the universal
devours each particular, each life
reduced to its essential. What
can I know
is not a question.

Of course I wanted power, I wanted
the power to save not a civilization but
one small petal from its flower.

For in its perfect hour, it was lovely.
But not a week. Not even one whole day –
this perfect product of ten thousand
thousand years – perfection –

before a cleansing rain.
Before the hand
protects the heart
with its tight fist again.

## Conscientious Objection

As the years go by
the judges who condemn you grow in number;
as the years go by you converse with fewer voices, ...
     – SEFERIS


Human, // word like an archway, a bridge, an altar. ...
     – LEVERTOV


Those who rose up against arms so long ago rise up again
in anger, their voices strange and cold
sounding the names of Nicaragua and El Salvador
where, twenty years before, we sounded
together the names of Cambodia, Laos, and Viet Nam.

But I am dumb. Winter draws in its nets of silver.
Each day we draw more distant from the sun.
Sometimes we manage one small moment of epiphany –
a glimpse of greater harmony within –
but too soon turn back toward the paths we came from,

harsh in all our judgments, harsh in voice
and tone. "I will die," a poet once declared, "but that is
all that I will do for death." Like her, I too
will be counted among the living; I too stand against
the few who make a profit peddling death.

But I am numb. "When one's friends hate each other /
     how can there

be peace in the world?" A shard of sunlight
slicing through a cloud could never penetrate a heart
more deeply than the necessity to speak
directly, but I can't. I too have visited the dead.

I counted friends among them. I counted
a few that almost made me glad. Herakleitos said
the thunderbolt will rule our lives, but he
is also dead and we are left among the monuments
to grieve. And to invent a Paradise.

———

There is a great sea called Tranquillity. I saw it once
on a map. There were white ships with white sails
blown by Adriatic breezes, there were cargoes of dream
and belief – I saw it all on the map.
But I could never take you there. I can't find it again.

But here is the sea I know, hard and cold,
bitter in its judgment, flattened by a sky of solid ash.
The day's news arrives with its nerves exposed
and we are hardened, our blood cools, and a ghost from
        the past
delivers our narcissistic sermon

in the same old monotone our parents heard at Auschwitz
or Treblinka. When summer comes, the sea
will turn to gold and we will see our reflected faces
in the water. Only then can we remember
the many-hearted rose opening, one after another,

its own most secret chambers to the end.
We walk on the ashes of the dead beneath a sky of ash.
The Japanese combine the word for *word*
with the word for *temple* to get the word for poetry:
temple word; holy word; no word can save.

But we all have wounds only a few right words can poultice.
We long all winter for summer's blue;
all summer we long for quiet. The voices we converse with
year by year grow fewer. In the Temple of the Dead,
speak softly. And if you must speak, praise.

———

Those who rose in protest long ago rise up again.
I who am brother to dragons and friend
to the hosts of the dead have tuned my harp for mourning:
I listen for sobs in the night. Black ships
sail out on seas of solid black. Our bitter countrymen

can't hear the winds that blow, can't see the knives
that slice our hands, can't taste the salt of seas we weep
          forever.
Our children grow older, early, older
than we will ever be. In the true country of the heart,
the dead rise up again, they rise and sing.

But we are not the dead. This sky of ash is cold and gray
above us, the earth itself is gray.
It's January. We miss the sweet stench of flowers.

The winter sun has gone where winter suns
all go: south into the sea. The world is a cell door slammed

against our faces while we breathe the fetor
of burning human flesh that rises from our sea of need,
our oceans of desire. Someone brought me
a winter rose to lift me from this dolor. Simple gifts
overpower. Peace in El Salvador

lives in the price one pays for a single flower to give one's
friend or lover. The dead are borne in us.
We were born at Sarajevo, we were born at Yalta,
in Dresden, Hiroshima, Manhattan.
The Rabbi of Auschwitz bows, grateful for life's one altar.

# From the Bunkers

*Fort Worden State Park, Port Townsend*

The first three-quarters of its century,
not a single pair of civilian feet
traversed this high hard balcony
of natural stone, iron and concrete:

Guns. The largest, we are told, weighed
almost sixty tons. But although the rounds
resounded over waters on the Strait,
not a shot was ever fired in anger.

All through the war to end all war
and through that other, bigger, one,
someone stood, just as always before,
in hope and terror, watching the empty ocean.

Nothing happens here. Row after row
of military crosses mark the graves of those
who died of accidents, syphilis, or worse,
who died of honor or of the common cold.

There are still the myths, ghosts, and tales:
depression of the Nineties, the slave trade;
of other warring states before the white man came:
called Kilsid or Chimakum.

A foolish man might say it's in our blood,

that long recorded history of our need
to fortify, to train our guns
on anything that moves or breathes.

The birds don't understand. Teals scud
slowly down the Strait. Gulls cry out
for gulls. Quail in the underbrush
and the gentle song of a mourning dove.

Soldiers' bodies washed up along the shore
remain in graves, unnamed after all these years,
like heroes home from war.
The Harbor Defense is closed.

An eagle loafs by on huge tired wings.
Poor eagle, never to sing:
the single note of its piercing cry
echoes down a vast, twilit, indifferent sky.

## September Sowing

There are no birds and no flowers. The juncos have gone
into the heavy air of September, robins
vanished into wet trees and falling leaves, and even the gulls
have grown silent, turning toward the sea.

Only yesterday, there were forget-me-nots, small and blue
and impossibly good to see. Clover blossomed under bees,
scotch broom yellow as the sun, and wild blackberries
turning black from purple in the heat.

Now even the ravens have flown, the sky opaque
and mean. While rain streaks my window,
I sit with morning coffee, thinking how,
when weather's good, I harvest the fruits of the dead,

the way I remember Roethke, whom I never met,
down among tide pools, on hands and knees,
examining barnacles on rocks, small shells the sea
leaves along the beach; the way I remember Seferis,

whose language I couldn't even speak, the way he'd see
the garden of a sleepy Arab house changing shape
and know it as a single note in a symphony, a fragment
of song too large for any one man to sing.

First autumn rains make a tomb of every house,
erasing bird, beast, and flower alike,
writing "emptiness" across the worn slate sky

of winter. Like an old wound which has healed

poorly, and aches when the weather changes,
the newly dead remain among us, but
their voices can't be distinguished from the cries
of those still dying. The old ones speak out singly.

Now, with rain continuing to fall
and my coffee cold in its cup and the small garden
turning dark, I think I can hear them again, faintly,
beyond the trees, beyond the cemetery stones,

beyond the clatter we set up to protect our ears
from the whispers of the dead. We live between mountains
and sea, between the music of the dead
and our own cacophony, between our own small fears

and huge collective dread. The garden
will rise up out of the sea.
The sky will warm and clear. And we will suddenly believe
our dreams and lives are one,

that we are here just once,
if only for a moment, but we are here,
drawing our lives and language from the dead,
living our deaths together.

———

Rain. Slowly. Steadily. Long morning rain,
then falling mist in a heavy haze out over the water,

western mountains a watercolor
mists will soon wash away. And only then,

late in the day, the sun breaks through
a crack in drifting clouds, the low plaintive wail
of sea-horns off in the Sound, and the sudden
gull-cry, shrill, lonely, slicing

a soft autumn sky. With the sun
slipping through trees, our little Japanese garden
takes on a shadowy yellow glow,
budding groves of three-foot-high bamboo

looking strong, shining for the first time
since early April. I draw each breath slowly,
like drawing water from a well,
and the sun is gone, drowned, its fingertips

lingering in treetops, the earth below
returned to rich greens and shadows,
black to gray. And what is a life, and what
have I done, and what, after all, is a day?

A broken line of geese, black and silent,
wavering southward down the sky,
a brush-stroke reminding me of old Tu
"adrift between earth and heaven," his eyes

forever rising from earth to horizon
or dropping from the wide heights of heaven
to the skyline. A day in September

every September for the past twelve hundred years.

That kind old Chinese gentleman would understand,
he himself looking back at least that far again:
the same winds blow in from the sea,
blowing *yang*, then *yin*,

the same lonely gulls wandering the tides:
you can hear them call and call again.
Age-old cedars creak and bend
as they have since time began.

The same worn clouds overhead. The same sun.
It is only a day in a life, you will say,
more a footnote than a song.
But the same winter comes.

———

Every September dawn and dusk is like
the twilight of the world.
Praise the autumn evening: the dark
will be truly dark.

Not like in the city where artificial twilight
lasts forever; not like the city's
infinite hum and strings of lonely lights
burning alone in shadows

where true darkness never comes.
When last light pales the west, there is

neither fear nor sadness,
only a memory of a mild September day

as a way of knowing, a kind of learning
through mnemonics, memorizing the rhythm
of the tides, of the day, and of the seasons.
It is a way of sowing fields left fallow in the mind.

Here, waiting alone in failing light,
I realize that for most of America
it is already night. Venus stirs in the west.
Soon, I will see Kueh Hsing

hiding in the Dipper. The stars called
Cowboy and Weaving Girl
enjoy their annual reunion
high over the Yangtze River.

Blue seawater fills our veins and stars float there
in the trade winds of the heart.
Here on the edge of the floating world,
I scratch out a kind of life

from rich soil and stone piled thin
on a ridge of basalt risen from the ocean.
Winter winds blow in from China and Japan.
I think the sky must be clearing.

They tell me everything grows simple
toward the end. I've wasted forty years
watching nothing out of windows, and I can't pretend:

whatever it was I've done, I did it, finally,

wrong – wanting perhaps not something
as simple as a song, I tried to join my voice
to others, but they all sang alone. I wanted
to marry my voice to a chorus,

but this life cannot be made into a scene
from old Euripides. I feel my daughter
swimming through my blood against a tide
as certain as the sea's. By the time

she reaches me, I'm gone. She, too, will listen
to hypnotic witcheries on the wind,
she, too, will listen to the dead
to learn her song.

———

Child I tore from a dream and wrenched into this world,
only blood of my blood, I adore you.
And never more than now:
we walk this path of rain and wind

listening to the dialogue between the Antiphonist
and Mary of the Clouds, you with blue beads
from Pandrosou Street and many earrings, I,
listening for the breath, the heart, for any sign

of tenderness, each of us
remembering islands of plane trees and olive groves,

the great harbor at Rodos
the Colossus carefully guarded

until *he* fell, mortal, into the blue Aegean Sea.
We too will fall. In time. But now,
night coming on with its arms full of stars
and memories, there are the ancient night-sounds

we name but cannot know, the dizzying whirl
of heavens overhead, the soft
almost human noises muttered by the lonely
as they turn, alone, toward bed.

It is finally dark. Our little garden closes
in the last hint of light, shadows drowning shadows,
wild roses and vine maple and English ivy
and thick, dense salal all turning

into a rich quilt of black brocade as I speak.
There are no birds and no flowers.
Only that sweet nostalgia for clover
humming with bees.

Alive, we harvest the fruits of the dead
together, our hearts changing shape,
growing smaller or larger, forever threatening
to break.

And what is a life? And what is a day?
An old man's loneliness which can't be shared.
A young woman's works and dreams.

And a spark of light between.

The things we've seen, we never came to know.
And those we know, we never truly see.
September swells the tides. It's a humbling glory:
a poor man's life is metaphor.

## Friend

It's barely October, but almost
overnight, it's autumn.

A few lank strands of sunlight
dangle through the clouds.

The hawks stopped circling meadows
and moved toward trees where varmints nest

building secret places for the winter.
Days grow fainter, shadows last forever.

I would like to sit outside today,
to drag my rocker out to the deck and sit

and listen to your stories.
I would like to sit outside in my rocker

and pour you a glass of bourbon.
See, back in that corner,

in the shadows of that cedar,
you see that small Jap maple?

It turned yellow and red last Tuesday.
Monday, it was vermilion.

I love that goddamned tree. Autumn here
is otherwise so subtle.

But good storytelling weather – cool
enough in the evening to enjoy a little fire,

a morning chill
to stir the blood to labor.

Oh, it's not the sun I worship,
but the hour. For now, sit here.

It is a kindness when
old friends can be together, quiet.

This fine October air is ours,
friend, to share. Contemplation

is both our gentlest
and our most awesome power.

## With the Gift of a Nootka Rose

The trill of thrushes, almost unnoticed,
there, at the edge of deepening shadows
in the shrubbery, sadly,

and the last Nootka roses,
once bright, their pink blossoms fading slowly in the sun,
"have the look of flowers that are looked at."

And there's a wilting in us,
a draining away like color from wild roses, a little song
like the three pathetic notes a robin drops
from the topmost boughs of cedar.

I cannot understand
how the shape of a flower
can break a heart in two, or how a robin on a summer day
can take my breath away.

Do you remember, years ago,
you brought me a small white
tightly shuttered rose
in a small white vase
with a single spray
of baby's breath. We had quarreled, perhaps,

I had said something ugly,
and you brought me,
you said,

a rose.
In lieu of an olive bough.

———

And now, remembering, sun straight and high and still,
and the singular self moving on, westward
toward the last mountains
settling into the western sea,
north toward the cold white emptiness of knowing –
the self is constantly moving.

And now, years later, the beautiful white blossoms
of ocean spray
turn dingy summer yellow.

I'd sooner give my heart to ocean spray
or to this Nootka rose
than to any American Beauty.

I want to
bring you this wild rose to remind you of the rose
you brought me
so long ago,
a time when I had hurt you.

But surely it will die
before I can get it home.

So here I sit, lonely on a dusty summer trail,
dying from the inside out,

strangling on my own heart's own in-
articulate tongue.
Drowning in my own language.

———

For days it has hung
over everything, this emptiness, this sweltering thing
that drains the color from our words
and lends them a useless ring, this clammy hand
damaging my sleep.

No wind to trouble the summer's dust.
A plump garden spider builds her bridge
from thistle to thistle
where she will nest. Long-suffering thrushes
slip from shadow to shadow
through the trees. The finches
get drunk on plums and sing.

Sometimes we are blown
like dry husks. Sometimes we can remember
only that the sea is salt and dead.
If I came to you now, we would place
our silence between us on the table
like cold gruel, our bread and our water,
until even the night couldn't heal us.

For the gift of a Nootka rose,
I would get on my knees
and beg
if only I knew how.

But dust has settled the summer.
You brought me a rose
long ago when I hurt you.
I loved you
when I was still a child.


———


And now, evening coming on, last light
sailing slowly out to sea, last birds grown quiet,
vanishing into the trees, the sky blue-purple and the
    first stars
drifting over hills to the east,

I strip my last cigarette
and get up from this rotting stump
I've perched on half my life, it seems,
get up, and start back home
with a fading rose in my pocket.

My shadow lies splayed
behind me like my past.
Not a sound in all the world. Even the gulls have gone,
and the shadows of trees fall over our house
like huge, lonely hands.

Beside the incense burner,
I lay a dying rose
and light a cone of musk. A spider's thread of smoke
    curls up
through the open, empty hands
of Kannon:

bodhisattva of compassion,
goddess of mercy,
deliver us.

# Unforgiven

From the sea, this sea
of green trees
appears deep blue,

a huge, gentle
tsunami
by Hokusai.

Thus we sink into
ourselves, stones
through water,

coming to rest
in the perfect calm
of the unforgiving world.

## A Photograph of Kavafis

Kavafis wears a dark, striped suit. He is seated
at the end of a couch, uncomfortably, his knees
together, his heavy, ankle-high shoes places carefully
on the floor before him like two objects, one
forearm thrown over his lap like an afterthought,

his eyes looking into the floor just beyond his feet,
the lids heavy, sagging as if from the weight
of history's ghosts. His jaw set, his lips pursed sadly.
Behind him on the wall, a Ming tapestry tells
the story of a once-great prince, and of the love he lost.

## Classical Tragedy

As long as the day lasts, it will not last
long enough. The legions of the rain
ride forward in their chariots, the dark comes on.
Still, there is time enough for the sun
to light the bare brown shoulders of a girl
glancing back down a country road,
time for the click, the buzz and hum
of summer insects in her hair.

Lying in the sun with the tragedies of Iphigenia
and Antigone, the day will not last long enough
for me to understand the breezes
in the trees or the clouds above. Sometimes
a robin sings. But when it rains,
we lift our faces up, remembering the sun
that turned our world to dust. As if
we expected the day, for a moment, to remember us.

## Listen, Ianni

We are ruled by thunderbolts, as Herakleitos said.
All night, thunderbolts rumbled over the Aegean,
thunderbolts lighting the sky high over the crumbling
        temple
of Lindean Athene.

Now in the gray afternoon, rain still falls as though
it could wash away October. Listen, Ianni, to water
        running
through the streets, how it adores the flat, worn stones
        we've exhausted
with the centuries of our walking.

The gods have all vanished. And still we search
for a Helen.
To east or west, the old news remains new:
death in Grenada, death in Kypros, death in Lebanon.

And we pause to honor Okhi Day
when the Greeks said No to the Axis. Because it is better
        to die
than to live without life. And we say No again
because someone didn't listen, because someone

needs a martyr, because the saints, like the gods,
are dead. Because tomorrow, after the rain has washed
        away our shame,

we'll have to begin again to build
a simple home for Helen. Wherever we go,

we walk on the faces of the dead.
Old women dress in black to mourn their dying Christ.
Everything gets ground into stars and stories, the day's
    birth and death,
the love all children have that we can't take away.

Listen, Ianni: let me fill your glass. This world
will too soon pass us by. Be still. Listen
to the sweet, sweet Mediterranean rain
dripping through the leaves of the pomegranate tree.

# Historical Romance

## I. ALIS UBBO

Hard rain pummels the Avenida da Liberdade.
The Rio Tejo is swollen
dark with silt and new hillside soil.
This same rain fell on the Phoenicians
who called this
"Delightful Little Port"
so many hundreds of years ago.

Even the beggars in the Praça do Rossio
have clothed their twisted limbs
and gone wherever beggars go.

We walk beside the Fountain of Maximilian,
rounding the square,
three of us arm in arm,
unaware that by morning
the Algarve would be closed,
the Costa Verde
a veritable island,
all bridges north and south
swept away downstream or out into the Atlantic.

Perched on its topmost hill
and growing darker by the hour,
the old gray stone Alfama,
eight stony centuries of blood
blackening its towers. We climb

the high walls and walk
its perimeter together,
pausing to search the city
from dank parapets at its corners.

Nothing but poor, black-shawled women
hanging out their laundry in the alleyways
of tenements,
nothing but a few old men with canes
and memories of war,
nothing but a few dirty children
throwing stones at alley cats or running through the rain.
Nothing changed in eight hundred years
but the bare-bulb glow of shabby rooms
one afternoon in autumn.

The same bread soup bubbles on a stove.
The same streets reek of fish and urine.
The same gray light stains everything it touches,
rich and poor alike.

A few swallows sail in the rain
over black slate roofs
as they did over Moors and Romans.
Barges and boats float slowly
down the huge brown river, round the bend,
and vanish.

We who have traveled across centuries
from a world we think is new
think this poverty is nostalgia,
that we don't belong to it.

My daughter speaks to them by name
and tells them about Brazil.
Because it is far away,
they think it must be better.

And we go back through evening light
and heavy rain,
back to our hotel to drink alone in the bar.

My daughter takes my face in her hands
and holds it like a mother: Don't worry,
she says, tomorrow we'll take the train
to Evora –
it's the only line that's left.

And my partner says,
And if that's not enough,
we can ride the bus all day – those hard-backed seats –
and take in a *juerga* in Seville,
we can visit the Moorish gardens in the Alcazar
and search the bookstalls Saturday
for Spanish editions of Lorca and Alberti.

And if it's literary history you crave,
we'll take a single yellow rose
to throw into the river
for all the Spanish poets
who haven't any graves.

*Laborare est orare.*
Saint Francis, forgive them.
How can they know what they do?
– Pillars of skulls,
walls of human bones,
and in your name, they pray.

When I asked the old priest I'd spoken with on the street
how this chapel came to be built,
he pretended he didn't speak English;
and when my daughter asked
in pure, clear Portuguese,
he said he didn't know.

We stood inside a whole afternoon
in a silence heavy as syrup, the bones of the fearful
or of the unafraid
five hundred years locked in plaster,
five hundred years, and the terror they promise
is eternal.

Outside the rain continued to fall.
Someone came in, knelt before the little altar,
and lit a single candle.
Being pantheist and pagan,
we knew it was time to go.

All night, hammer-blows of rain rang on cobblestones.
Cold in the Spanish dark,

I screamed myself awake,
dreams of fire and bones and blood
shattering my sleep.

To the south and the west, there are seas,
calm beaches, gentle evening breezes in the olive groves,
a history of so long ago it seems
almost a mercy, a pain so remote
we think we can embrace it,
naming it History, or Hellenism, or Love.

I cannot sleep.
"Labor *is* prayer,"
Tree repeats, and says a chapel built of bones
is a natural thing.
The temple, she says,
is neither in the bones nor of them:
they are the instrument through which it sings.

### III. PLAZA DE ESPAÑA, SEVILLA

Riding all day on a cold bus through broken fields
and hills of wild flowers,
past relics of failed rancheros, there were birds we
    couldn't name
slumping down gray skies
above huge, black Andalusian bulls
standing aloof and dark,
watching nothing, like sullen, indifferent gods
about to embrace their wounds.

And then evening coming on and the first glimmer
of sunlight in a week,
rolling down from easy hills, city lights
soft in the east like sunrise,
the city before us like a postcard from the country
of a dream:
huge cathedral black against the sky,
its bell-tower lit from below
like a masked face on Halloween
with a candle beneath the chin
to frighten all the children.

We eat gazpacho and chorizo and wander city streets
like any good *turista*. The Torre del Oro
rises dark and shining
from the banks of the Guadalquivir,
and everywhere, we think, we hear music:

and I want,
suddenly,
to learn the names of all the flowers in Spanish,
I want to visit
my ancestor's grave in Venice,
to bring him one defeated rose from Spain.

Turning back down narrow corridors leading toward
        our room,
our feet, unaccustomed to cobblestone,
ache and ache.

And something else,
inside,
cold and hard
like a stone inside the heart.
But just before I fall asleep,
I think: Sevilla,…Sevilla,…
and call it softly, feeling with my mouth, –
*Sevilla,…Sevilla,…*
thinking it harsh and beautiful, beautiful and harsh
like love.

———

Dawn arrives with its wagonload of gold –
a clatter in the streets below,
and yellow sun so bright
even fine gauze curtains
can't protect my eyes.

The night's waves washed over me
and carried me out again into dream:
a memory of music in the hills,
distant music and bawling sheep,
an old man with stubble on his chin
remembering the guns, the black boots of the
    Generalissimo
on the plaza forty-five years ago.

Walking in warm December sun
between two lovely women, why must I remember
only dreams of martyrs,

our unaccountable failures,
our national greed?

The great cathedral built on the wreckage of a mosque
tolls the morning hour:
nine o'clock.
By ten, we're in the plaza:
the river, still and blue,
curls slowly under bridges
along the colonnade.

We walk along
looking at coats-of-arms
remembering what we can
of the failed revolution
until we come
to the Capitania General:

two military guards with burp-guns
stand outside the hall.
The first steps forward
and waves us on our way.
His eyes are dead.

Beyond the river, in the Parque de Maria Luisa,
there are jasmine and rose-trees,
narrow lanes among fountains,
and a monument
to the poet Gustavo Adolfo Bequer,
complete with Cupid and swooning girls –
the dream of a past before the past we see.

Soon, we will fly all night
in a drone above the Atlantic.
We will bring back everything we were given.

Who has heard the sound of boot-heels echo
on the flesh-colored tile of the plaza

will remember.
And remember roses in December
purchased from a pushcart in the plaza,

and the myrtle labyrinth
and infinite corridors
of the Alcazar.

It is autumn in a city we have dreamed.

The maple leaves are turning red, the night
grows long and cold.

We will fly west until we vanish in the sun.

It is beautiful and sad
the way we,
dying,

make monuments of the dead.

# The Uta Mound

Dusk, the Omi Sea,
a lone plover skimming waves,
and with each soft cry
my heart too, like dwarf bamboo,
stirred, longing for bygone days.

– KAKINOMOTO NO HITOMARO

Ruined capitals
at Omi and Yoshino
long since turned to dust.
Sunlight sets fields ablaze
in cold eastern dawn;
facing west, the moon returns
to its hilltop grave.
He who walked the Aki fields
knows eternal rest
deep within the Uta Mound,
ancient Yamato
protected by wide mountains,
Fujiwara gods,
and by Hitomaro's songs.

The Empress Jitō
still haunts Yoshino fields,
a pale, aging ghost
mourning her husband and son,
wandering mountains
and slow crystalline rivers

where her palace stood,
boats on the morning water
strewn with spring blossoms,
cormorants fishing shallows
wrapped in mists of time.
No more than a dream remains –
the Empress, the song
from a time no one can know.

When he left his wife
at Tsuno Cove in Iwami,
winds took morning wings
and the waves took evening wings
singing in his ears
like thunder throwing offing;
and at Cape Kara
on the Sea of Iwami,
the sway of seaweed
like the sway of love he longed
to feel in his arms
again, Hitomaro rode
to the capital
alone with the lonely moon.

At Sento-Gosho,
beyond Omiya Palace
and Akose Pool,
the rockery, Tosa Bridge,
islands in the pond
where royalty strolled and dreamed –
at Sento-Gosho,

just beyond the gray stone shore,
South Pond's Dreary Beach,
beyond Seikatei Teahouse,
the poet's shrine: small,
quiet. Almost no one comes.
Just a man in sum.
But among Man'yōshu poets,
almost a god, a sovereign.

*Sedoka*

Kakinomoto
no Hitomaro, poet.
Nothing to learn of the man.
Dusty worn old shrine.
He walks in *komoriku*,
he wanders the hidden land.

# Two Poems for Tanabata Matsuri

## 1. Altair and Vega

Spring has gone. The brief hour
of cherry blossom time
passed again into the heart's mind
which revises and refines
momentary loves
that last longer than a lifetime.

Spring has gone again,
and once again, *kumo no umi* –
a sea of clouds
darkens the rainy season.
The paper sags
on the shoji screens.

Even inside the house,
the washed clothes won't dry,
new books begin to mildew,
bedding damp all night.
Then comes July,
a swelter, a stifling light.

But it is Seven/Seven,
Altair and Vega meet again
high above the Yangtze.
Once each year the Cowboy, Kengyu,
returns to his lover,
Shokujo, the Weaving Girl.

In the topography of the heart
it is the hour of vistas,
it is the hour of seeing deeply
into the warm night's core:
what happens here now
has happened a billion times before.

What is a river
between two lovers, what is a sea
to cross, what is the Milky Way
but a river of stars
pouring down from heaven?
Come here, beside me.

That love which seeks love
is only a human affection.
Stars drift and shine and intertwine
only in our eyes.
Being itself becomes a metaphor.
"Meaning" has no meaning.

Altair and Vega, Kengyu and Shokujo, –
the story of love divided
is the story of every love.
The end of the story
is neither happy nor tragic.
Like Altair and Vega,

we ride the night sky alone,
reflecting only the light
which shines on us
from other burning stars.

Be still. Stay a moment
just as you are.

It is the seventh day
of the seventh month –
the mundane world
lies millions of miles away.
Let me undress you slowly
by the light of the Milky Way.

We burst into flame,
burning through the night.
It is a dream of water,
of galaxies in flight,
it is the story of the Phoenix,
it is a sea of dream, an ocean of delight.

Let me kiss your mouth
and breathe the scent of your hair.
I love you cautiously, slowly,
deeply, like a river under the stars,
like the river
reflecting Vega and Altair.

2. SWEATING IT OUT

after Tanabata Festival,
written in the margins
of the *Man'yōshu*

There is nothing elegant
about sweat.

The gray dawn breaks
over Musashino Plain
and a few small raindrops fall.
The dust is not stirred,
                            the birds
are almost silent: sparrow-
chirps, but no doves, no magpies.
Even the crows grow silent
in this swelter.
                    At my desk,
sitting in my shorts,
                            shirtless,
ten minutes from the shower,
skin clings to skin, a thick glaze
coating the body.
                    Here I sit,
reading Prince Aki's *choka*
in the *Man'yōshu*, wasting
my life on poetry, dreams
of spring rain,
                    the tormented
songs of a people spoken
in a voice at once human
and humane.
                    Prince Aki
loved a woman
                    he was not
supposed to love, a woman
forbidden, one far beneath
his station. Separated
by imperial
                    command,

he longed for clouds and rain, for
the wings of a bird to fly, for
a few gentle words to speak

a plain and elegant truth.

———

A few perspiration drops
stain the page as I read. Twelve
hundred years have vanished in
a single moment.
               The stars
called Cowboy and Weaving Girl
meet high over the River
of Heaven, crossing the bridge
of magpies.
            Tanabata
Matsuri passes without
a poem, streamers hung
in the city streets are made
of plastic,
           and the lovers
who stood on the bridge and dreamed
of arms out-stretched for pillows
have vanished in the water.

No moon.
          Only the swelter
of Yamato in July,
only the same ageless dream
of crossing Heaven's River.

What do they mean, those old songs
of love and sorrow?
                 The years
have not changed.
                  We have not changed
ourselves. We also love dreams
of dreaming, a lover's song
of parting and denial,
of hope in deep affection.

And still, there is no meaning.
Here, sweating over a song
a thousand years old, I come
into myself: the heart's music
has not changed in a thousand
thousand years.
               Being is enough.
To love,
       plenty. The past is not
over, it is becoming.

*Envoy*

A new year begins.
Every morning this morning.
Every day begins today.
Another year passed.
Sunlight. Clouds. Birds on the wing.
Only this moment. At last.

## Organic Form

A year on one line,
searching for the poetry:
outside, breezes rise –
spring to summer to autumn –
leaves fall, rot, and feed the tree.

## Mountains and Rivers without End

After making love, we are like
rivers come down from mountain summits.

We are still, we are moving,
calm in the depths of danger –

two rivers entering the sea
slowly, as if nothing matters:

quietly, but with great power,
merging in deepening waters.

# Ten Thousand Sutras

*after Hakuin*

The body is the body of the Buddha.
Like ice and water, the one is always in the other.

In the middle of the lake
we long for a drink of water.

Adrift in Samsara
we dream of blissful Nirvana.

This body is the body of the Buddha,
this moment an eternity.

Saying *I love you*, the deed is done –
the name and the deed are one.

With you and without you
the line runs straight –

your body is the body of the Buddha,
there is light beyond the gate.

This love I give to you
is the love that comes from Kannon.

Every breath a sutra.
Going or returning, it's the same.

Our bodies are the bodies of the Buddha,
our names are Kannon's name.

No word can adequately say it,
yet every word must praise it –

in silent meditation
destroying evil karma,
in silent meditation
inhabiting the Dharma –

this body is the body of the Buddha,
your body is the body of the Buddha.

Open arms and eyes to Samsara!
Embraced by the thousand arms of Kannon!

In the perfect mind of vivikta-dharma,
the truth of solitude,

our body is a temple
not a refuge.

Praise our body
even in Samsara,

our bodies are the body of the Buddha,
our bodies are the body of the Buddha.

# Kannon

I adore you. I love you
completely. Nothing to ask in return.

Each act of affection a lesson:
I fail, but with each failure, learn.

Like studying
under Te-shan:

thirty blows if I can't answer,
thirty blows if I can.

# Watching the Waves

For fifty years I've drifted,
carried on wandering waves
like a single grain of sand
from a beach a world away.

Yun-men raised his dragon staff:
it swallowed earth and heaven.
Gills and scales at Dragon Gate,
all these years chasing waves!

You return to your cottage
nestled in northern mountains.
I remain in the city,
red dust burning in my eyes.

Moonlight troubles the waters;
mountains and rivers remain.
Blinding light every morning;
in the evening, clouds and rain.

IV.

## Arse Poetica

You stand like a twin-headed bird,
one head open-mouthed in song,
the other stitched tight in sorrow.
An odd dance of *yin* and *yang*.

You simply cannot escape
your own original face.
The Greeks called this
excessive ego *hubris,*

consequence of the sin being
violence brought down
upon one's own head:
*karma* – pride's other twin.

Charmed, the storyteller
is always surprised
by the hard truths
of his own enchanting lies.

As one might, perhaps, come
to Literature – capital L –
only to find – what in hell?
Geoffrey Chaucer's bare red bum.

## "Io no piangeva;

*si dentro impietrai.*
*Piangevan elli"* –

Dante's Ugolino,
recounting his suffering.

Because he could not wail,
he turned to stone inside.

Seferis on the riverbank
wanted only to speak simply,

"to be granted that grace."
Three hundred thousand tons

of non-biodegradable DDT
delivered into the watershed.

What we have done
cannot be undone.

Our silence turns
every heart to stone,

our ability to speak simply
lost, disgraced

by lies and misplaced
loyalties to false wealth

disguised
by more private and official lies.

# Malebolge: Prince William Sound

"This world knows them as a blind people,
greedy, invidious, and arrogant;
cleanse yourself of their foul ways."

– Ser Brunetto Latini to Dante,
in the bowels of Hell's seventh circle,
and he named them:
*gent' è avara, invidiosa e superba.*

And Brunetto said, "Know that I keep company
with clerics and with the literati
and with those who know grand fame,
and for each, the sin against earth is the same."

And going deeper, Virgil used Dante's belt
to summon Geryon from the depths,
to carry them on his back to the edge of Malebolge
where flatterers are immersed in excrement.

Teals. Terns. Eagle and raven. Sea otter, clam, and salmon.
The world's tallest mountains
are all under water. Porcupine, beaver, muskrat.
Brown bear and black bear and tiny brown bat.

The people of the soil – call us *human* anyway –
linger at the shore. We are only humus.
Bear and otter no longer out-swim us.
Loon, hawk, and wild goose no longer fly away.

Opening the heart's own book,
look! there's Dante in a man-made Hell,
entering Malebolge on the back of the beast he dreamed,
there are rivers of blood and misery;

there's old blind Homer
listening as tales of Odysseus wind and unfold;
there are tales of Tlingit and Haida and Kwakiutl;
the dance of Krishna, eighth avatar of Vishnu.

But nothing prepares the blood to assume
this speechlessness, profound silence of complete grief,
this vision of hell we can't escape
unfolding before our eyes.

Strangling on our own greedy, greasy lies,
the thick black blood of the ancient world
covers and clogs our lives.
What can be washed away is washed away

like history, tar-balls riding out the tides.
We turn back to our own anthropomorphic needs,
our creature comforts, our poems and our famous lies,
closing the book on Homer, Dante, and Brunetti,

closing the book of the heart
on the face of god, and on her counterpart:
rock, fish, bird, plant, and beast:
on you, on me, and on the Geryon we ride: Exxon Valdez.

175

# Blue Monody

*Blues for Thomas McGrath*

And now the winds return,
blowing in from the sea,
driving summer steadily away,
south toward tall palms
we dreamed of when we were children
shivering in snows
that never ended.

And now these winds return
with frozen hands and laughter,
tormenting mountains,
twisting trees until you think
that like any human heart
they cannot bend farther
and will surely break.

I've kept my heart in my hands
through all these storms and seasons.
I've held it tight.
When the great trees bend
and their groans are almost human,
I've looked up more than once
from the desk where I invent a life,
looked up stunned
when they cried out,
thinking it a friend

arrived for comfort in the cold,
or my own harsh voice
grown suddenly old and fearful,

the fitful cry of a man whose name
was never counted
among the names of the innocent

and now must face the winter.

I've held my heart
in my hands and pushed
my breath across it
to blow the snow away.

Traveling, traveling, I've learned
a few exotic names
and places where great deaths occurred,
where the lonely are buried in their trenches,
in mass graves which couldn't,
under all that earth,
disguise the misery carved
into ordinary faces.

The winds continue to grieve
although the dead ask nothing
from us now. And nothing
is what we gave:
I've held tight
to this heart I could not break
like an egg to eat.

The wounds, the wounds I bore
were not my own,
but this hunger is all mine.

These trees, defeated by the wind,
endure: they cling to the earth
and won't let go
despite sea-winds drumming blows.

———

Down in the bay, the old wharf
slowly crumbles,
gray wood bleached almost white,
huge timbers ruptured.

Homer thought a field of lovely asphodels
would mark the homelands of the dead, but we know
differently, having seen
those faces rising from the sea
a thousand times or more,
their own chewed hearts
rotting in their hands, each
marching slowly inland
with his broken oar.

No matter how far inland we may stray,
we can't escape the sea.
Each heart longs to be
Odysseus, to bear its wounds
forthrightly,

long enough not to survive,
but to embrace,
if only once again,
Penelope.

Here on a gnarled coast, winds
play cruel jokes, twisting trees
into almost human forms
reminding us of nothing
so much as our own brutality.

Cold September winds blow in from the stormy sea.
I've got my heart in my hands again.

If you pass by, do not think that I
am not afraid.
Winds will drive me down beneath the waves,
under ravaged trees I cannot save.

They are neither laurel nor myrtle;
nor am I
a Milton;
nor you
a Lycidas, nor dead.

Here is the wreckage of a heart:
take it from my hands.
No one understands
the winds or the sea. We mourn because
we are alive. I give you this monody.

———

It is true, as the poet sang, Elder Brother:
*Every angel terrifies.*
I've never seen an angel, but I've heard
those cries of a desperate cat,
bawling with and without her Tom,
the sexual need to scream
the soul's desire, the cries
we all come from…

every angel terrifies. Because
there is also
always a little ugliness inside,
every angel terrifies.

The deep sexual wail of the alley cat
is purest song: uncluttered by metaphor or meaning,
it says nothing but what it is –
the single note of desire without cunning,
its only meaning *being* –
– we confuse the sound; we have our self-
deceptions to consider – we
who are burdened with enormous
intentions to remember.

Everyone is desperate,
singing solo.

Night comes down hard
and we turn alone in bed
toward bare needs we'd meant
to leave behind.

We listen to the dark
and hear only winds and waves
that never stop.
Somewhere
between nightmare and insomnia,
stars conspire to wink and shine.

Old Compañero, I tell you,
the thought of singing solo
terrifies:

Bird on the hill,
little cricket
itching in the grass,...

...bitterness like a razor on the tongue...
...it is hard, brother,
seeing those blank faces
of battered mothers
at the marketplace, hard looking into empty eyes
of children who die
a little every night.

"The soul
to know itself
must look into a soul" –
and sing.
There is always
that old eternal
other side of things –
which brings us

to our knees.

A mirror is not a soul. It's not
for daily trivialities,
not even for our own
self-centered lone-
liness that we listen
at the heart of things.

Stoked on drugs
and driving at light-speed
down a dead-end street,
there's barely time to think.
What terrifies most deeply
is what we see
inside: every angel
driven out by lies.

Jeezus-gawd-aw-mighty, there were angels in your eyes!

Imagine Hoover
waking alone in the night,
thinking hard on your fate,
on the fate of your sisters and brothers, –
flat-nosed, square-jawed, no-neck bigot
swirling into vertigo,
nauseous,
choking on his own poison phlegm,
cursing, "*Nigger! Kike!*"
as the faces (black and white)
march past him:

his allies:
the Senator from Wisconsin,
Joe McCarthy, and his cronies,
Bobby Kennedy and Richard Milhous Nixon;

and the House Committee
on Un-
American Activities

– a Commie in every bed,
a socialist in every bath –

and those who made the Blacklist,
not least of all
that proletarian angel, Tom McGrath.

Hoover sweats and clutches his heart
and tries to focus on his night-light.
The angels of dead civil rights
workers march slowly, inevitably by,
bloody, marching toward breaking daylight in the east.

…Confluences, visitations,
demon ghosts of the present arrive here from the past.

The Ghost of Christmas Present?

There is no peace.
And every angel terrifies.

———

Is that it?
Carbuncles on the skin of the body
politic?

Ten years ago,
snug in his little house
on this high, wind-blistered bluff,
low fire in the stove despite
it being midsummer
in the Northwest,

Tom McGrath sank deep into his chair
and turned warm eyes
opaquely back on time
to remember thorny years
lost in the depths
of "hornacle mines"
winding labyrinths
deep beneath
the infected and infesting streets
of the City of Lost Angels

until at last he escaped into
the long bleak night of the frozen north,
leaving Marsh Street [*Marsh* Street? In L.A.?]
leaving Marsh Street
and the hornacle mines behind,
and entered the thirty-year Christmas
of his wild American dream-dance
imagining a friend.

The Revolution lurched along somewhere
out there among rubbish
left behind
by pale men
who manned the picket lines.

Times were thin.

Hit lit a cigarette from a cigarette,
rolled his eyes, and grinned,
"K-e-e-e-rist,
you haven't seen anything
until you've seen the winds
sweep Moorhead
after the snow has frozen!
I swear you can *see* the cold!
Gawd, I'd hate to grow old up there."

From hornacle mine to beet-packing plant,
we followed,…
going down there over the river,…
alone,
over the river,…
over winter ice.

We were all lost together, gloriously
lost along the way,
searching for a heaven of blue stars,
building the Big Kachina…

And there it is
in the hexagrams
of yesterday's *I Ching*;
there it is,
written in piss in new winter snow beneath a cold blank sky
a thousand miles from nowhere,
a few miles down the road,
over the frozen river,
over winter ice....

To have power over Nature,
to have power over Bird and Forest,
over Sea and Mountain and Wild Beast,
to dream of power,
to cling to the dream of power in the hour
of greatest need:

to have stood silent
is to conspire, is to concede.

And now, a little south of here,
the white train rolls,
the white train regularly rolls.

"To be men, not destroyers,"
that was the task Grampa set,
learning from his own broken heart:
"wrong from the start, that stupid
suburban prejudice."

Stars caught in the bristling bare branches of trees
before the ice storm brought them down,
the earth frozen and black – the river
buried in shadow, no longer dreaming
a calm, indifferent sea,
a little ice along its edges:
it is time to face front,
get back on the line.

Strands of fog erase this stretch of beach,
swirls of fog erase the sky above the Sound.

To be takers, yes, to be sure;
but to be givers
also; to surrender
The Goods;
to be
searchers for the art
of the sublime – his sermon was the gift
of courage to face front and get back on the line.

Carbuncles on the cold skin
of the Body Politic.
The thin black shadow of a Trident Nuclear Sub
dices the vast Pacific.

To be men,
not destroyers,
that's the trick.

———

A gray night, just a few years ago,
we spent hours sipping on a beer,
remembering Michael Harrington,
his body wracked with cancer,
his soft, patient voice
over Public Radio
offering every moral answer
to Reagan/Bush agenda –
marching orders against the Sandinistas, –
and we toasted Norman Thomas,
Tom looking me in the eye
and asking how many will die
before the murders end,

and the jukebox of course
played a sad country song,
and he stood unsteadily, leaning on his cane,
and made a bad joke about Pound's posturing –
cane and cape and earring
during his early days in London
("the man wouldn't have been dumber
if he'd posed as Beau Brummel") –
and apologized for the music
"but not for the people –
'drather have a beer in here
than anywhere else in the country."

Dirty floors and haggard faces,
so many dreams pissed away.

Neither disgraced nor enlightened,

these were the men in the trenches,
the women who sent their sons to war,
who worked the factories,
and who paid taxes.

"Everything's in order," he said, and laughed,
"Some to die, some to be maimed,
everything is ready.
Everything's been done."

We cross the avenue:
"Helluva life when crossing a gutter's
the biggest challenge of the day!"
And he clutches my arm.

[Safe at his desk, door cozily bolted,
stealing a moment, another, higher, poet
peers out his window: two floors below,
the homeless go about their tasks,
and he records his heart to bursting,
he measures out his sympathies
before his lecture on form and epiphany –
probably at the expense of his graduate
seminar on Later Keats.]

The afternoon sun rides high above
the northern Mississippi.
A few cars slide by
as we walk slowly
under maple saplings in fluttering leaves
along clipped lawns in an autumn breeze.

Across the street, a man in greasy hand-me-downs
strides by with his sleeping roll.

"That one's been on the road
a while," Tom says,
"probably tryin' to find a train."

And we are a long way
outside Yellowstone
and a longer way from Port Townsend.
The things we've seen will never come again,
and who'd want to live them over?
And nothing changes.
The poor are the same poor, and the dead and the dying
are the same.

Where is the meaning? "Six million dead"
mean nothing to us – we who've only witnessed photos –
our abstracted, two-dimensional, superficial
        understanding.
And the seven million Russians, Estonians, Latvians,
        Lithuanians,
figures reaching ever-farther beyond
the ability of the mind to grasp?
Don't ask.

It is one thing to stand against murder,
and another to do without supper.
We stammer and cuss and blame one another.
The heavens continue to burn.

Somewhere in transit,
somewhere driving toward Pah-Gatzin-Kay or Boston,
crossing the Great Mountain, say,
that lies just outside of Moorhead,
the sound of the sea comes back to us
like the voice of long dead sailors,
familiar with its longing,
the hush of Puget Sound
when winds ride bluffs that rise above Fort Worden
and rattle the twisted limbs of brittle old madrona,
white flowers scattering to the winds,
winds,
when they return again each fall,
driving summer steadily away,
when all the winds and rains return with icy fingers,...

Homer thought a field of lovely asphodels would mark
the homelands of the dead.

What survives in the heart,
what endures,
lies just beneath what is said
when what is said
is said
*just so*:
only thus do we know
our own temple, our heaven, home
or hell.

Cisco Houston sang,

*You don't believe I'm leavin',*
*You can count the days I'm gone.*

———

Yellow alder leaves fall
where madrona blossoms,
small, delicate,
had fallen.

The grass grows tall and brown, and apples
 beckon yearling deer
who come down from wooded bluffs
to gorge until they're drunk.
Autumn fog tumbles along the water.
A few boats, a few seagulls –
like an amateur painting.

Sunlight slants away, turning yellow.

I've been sitting on the deck of the same bar on Water
 Street for hours,
ignoring my whiskey,
watching the changing dance of sunlight on the water
as the day or a lifetime passes,

and I remember how badly
I'd have wanted the whole damned bottle a few years ago
just to numb the aching,

and the whiskey-colored sun,

and its clattering light on the water,
my own self-pity
and the cry of the loon and the whine of a gull
and the toot of the out-going ferry.

I hang slack-jawed, empty,
a growing numbness just behind the eyes
although I am stone sober,

…sadness, melancholy,
or any of those other insufficient names we give to grieving,
or any of those other insufficient names we give to living,

while the puffins go on with their diving
and mountains in the distance turn black and then silver,
sky growing pale and growing wider.

A shadow grows over me and I shiver.

Poised at the edge of the sea
like a damaged bird,
I keep one eye
on each horizon: westward,
the vast implacable ocean
stitched to the wide indifferent sky;

to the east, mountains,
and beyond the mountains,
mountains, and the great rolling plains
where winds of change blow through our lives
like snows across the Dakotas, a cold blank nothing.

From the four corners of exile,
from the cracks and ravines of the ruptured human heart,
from the sea and the shadows of mountains,
a few friendly shadows,
a few friendly faces come back again
to taunt us, to lure us back on the line:

T'ao Ch'ien alone in his cabin
far from the intrigues of the city,
trying to give up the wine,
committed to his ploughing,
rests only at night to write poems
remembering his home on South Mountain;

sad, wise Tu Fu in exile,
alone at his brushwood gate, waiting to share his wine;
Saigyo gazing alone at the moon,
writing poem after poem;
Bashō and Ryōkan
alone on Sunset Hill
watching the River of Heaven pour down across Sado,
island of exiles in the Sea of Japan.

And I return to Helen,
exiled in Alexandria
while Troy burned.

Rexroth, exiled in Montecito
after forty years in The City,
wrote his best poems, love songs and elegies and his own
    epitaph.

What more could you ask? – a lifetime learning to speak
    simply.

When fame kneeled at the feet
of Georgia O'Keeffe, she, saintly, remained silent,
closed her door
and went on painting flower and bone and blank
pale sky, eighty-nine pages on file at the FBI.

Van Gogh, who couldn't peddle a painting,
saw only the same starry sky which demanded
he learn to speak
with his entire body – he too
listening with his eyes.

Down Port Townsend Bay,
the paper mill blows sulfur smoke in columns of soft
    white cloud
as the evening shift begins.

In town, it grows late.
The bric-a-brac shops and antique dealers,
the Rotary Club and Republican steering committee and
    Chamber of Commerce
and city offices close for the night again.
The day's decisions have been made
without the counsel of T'ao Ch'ien.
It's Friday night.
There's a football game.

———

And now the winds return, late,
to torment trees,
blowing autumn in from the sea.
These trees,
defeated by the wind, endure.

Faces rise through the night
as through water,
each with its blessing or its warning
we've heard a thousand times before,
each with its gift of hope and terror
we can't refuse,
each with its questions and its knowledge,
and the voices of trees groan or shriek in almost human
     form.

Exiled from the Garden,
this is the garden we murder and survive,
listening to days and seasons, to inconstant tides
and our own reflexive lies, refusing
to open our eyes to the enormous tragedy
of waterline and riverbed and darkened sky:

we struggle to re-invent the Garden with insecticides.

Pythagoras thought form
reflects
the irrational numerology
of Pure Mind. The Pure Mind of Buddhism
declares this world
illusion.

It is late.
The world sleeps or rises
or goes about its way. The wind blows.
The sea sighs. Someone once again,
at midnight,
opens the book of the heart.
A tree rattles and groans.

We are not in the dark.
We are not alone.

# Yellow Ribbons, Madness, Victory

While the nation welcomes home its heroes,
two hundred thousand corpses burn
and rot in the desert under billowing clouds
of oil smoke and mountains of rubble.
A pale moon at vernal equinox.
Wet snow falls on blossoming daffodils.

III:91

V.

# A Leaf

It is spring, full moon in a cloudless sky
after a long dark winter, a year after
another stupid war. Maybe these unconsoling stars
know the secret names of all we cannot know.

The mind turns in its hunger until it chews
the heart, that ruined badge of lovers.
And the stars are less vengeful than rueful.
And all the passing years rise slowly

from within until I am almost overcome
with loneliness and gratitude,
whatever it is that fills the breast
with hunger, with a river of longing.

The candle on the table gutters out in a flicker.
Turning on the lamp, I open a book of poems
to "Leaves," – as noble as Whitman's – and read
to myself alone. I am almost fifty.

# Abstract

It was a dream and you were walking through a field of
    hosannas
and the immense sea rocked with the blue voices of the dead
when you stretched out supine to dream lotus dreams which I
could not read.

A cathedral of sky arched overhead. I wanted to know
whether your eyes were closed, I wanted your dream or song
    or prayer,
oh I wanted, and the sun grew brighter and the breeze fairer
that immaculate day

unfolding like a poem, like a song I half-remember and ask,
Did we sing it once a long time ago, did we sing it together,
was it our hymnal, our beautiful tragic chorus, our anthem,
the day like a new white canvas,

and here I add marine blue, and there cobalt blue, and a cloud
    in amber,
and the light is transparent yellow, and the brush makes a sound
like wind over sand, but there are no whitecaps, no sailboats,
only canvas and paint and the body's dance.

No kite. No gull. No *things*. Everything goes.
No dream, no dreamer. No certainty, no doubt.
Only the infinitely blossoming hosannas of the emptiness
    within,
echoing the emptiness without.

# Destination Zero

Over low, rolling hills patch-worked by live oak
and post oak and maple,
and stitched with broken highways,
daybreak comes early, eastern sky
streaked with oranges and yellows that stir
the dove into song, that wake the mockingbird
who shakes the dew from white-tipped wings
and glides out over the fields to learn
whatever mockingbirds learn.

And I, too, have journeyed out of long darkness,
have risen
bewildered in the dark before dawn
in strange rooms smelling of smokestacks
in cities I could not name,
cities trembling beside plaintive trains that rumble through
on their long journey into memory,
I've risen to pull on the garments of this life like a
        mourning shroud
and walked out into first light
to test my own wet wings.

Is it dream or remembrance, this image
of myself behind the wheel on the arc of a long gray
        highway
winding from nowhere to nowhere,
any hills at all floating by,
a few clouds carried up

on the wings of wandering hawks,
and a heartland farmhouse crumbling on a ridge
above the rocky dry riverbed,
fields of stubble,
rusty fences and the sagging flatbed truck
someone used once long ago for baling hay, –

all my life driving into the dawn,
through the morning and down
long afternoons into corridors of stars,

driving past the freshly painted First Baptist Church
and the First Church of God
with its sagging foundation,
past the new brick First
Presbyterian Church that must own
the best scenic property in Heaven,
and the dirt-poor First Unitarian
clapboard church,
and the tidy First Methodist.

I am driving through "God's country" again.
Banks and churches cherish firstness.
The Bodhisattva
will be last to enter Nirvana.
It is daybreak and February in north Texas.
Daybreak shocks, it is so wide.

A mockingbird cries
and nothing moves.
A slip of smoke

from a chimney just beyond the hill.
Fine mist swirls and burns away.

All outward journeys run parallel
to the journey that leads in,
the self unfolding like petals on a rose,
opening one by one and falling
one by one
as we journey toward the center
that reveals only elemental emptiness within.

The arduous journey out of self is a journey toward the
     dawn.
So why, this late in life
and with a hundred years in these eyes,
must I travel with the weight of the dead again,
with relics from some other life
like a map I cannot read, destination zero.
The heritage of blood.

Orphaned in this world, as I have always been,
I have buried my dead
in God's country
again and again.
Lastness has been my way. Give me
an old man eyes, give me the silence
of the dead.
Lastness is my way.

At John Hall's farm in Mulberry, Texas,
I walked out to the pond,

paused to pluck a long gray feather
from a great blue heron's carcass –
shot by some witless kid –
it held the blue of the sky and nightfall gray
and the sound of the sea in its form.
But it was only a dead heron
like so many others,
putrid, buzzing flies.

Walking back across the fields, I watched
a crowd of cardinals gather in a tree,
the mockingbird called again and a ragged
old coyote zig-zagged into the wash below the hill,
warily,
not to be hung by his heels from a gate –
the way they do in God's country.

Little white-tailed mockingbird,
Saint Mimic
in the cathedral of Our Lady of Perpetual Longing,
little down-and-outer, God's dog,
tattered trickster,
show me the way.

I'm journeying out again,
don't ask me why,
soul spreading shabby feathers toward both edges
of the oncoming dawn,
embracing the breadth of
this endless sky.

II.

Snow falls lightly on my adoptive mother's
casket poised above
the gaping hole of her grave.
Suddenly, the sun breaks through
late February clouds with blinding yellow light.

She loved this land, Uintah,
Wasatch and La Sal mountain ranges
under snow, the striations
found in Wingate sandstone
in canyons near Moab, Utah,
where she was born
nearly ninety years ago.

And now she is dead with the one man
she loved, dead
with her love as with
her lies and denials.

My name was Arthur Brown
when first she lied to me –
for my own good, she always said –
driving me "home"
from the orphanage
to see my father and my dog.

"That's not my father,
and that's not my dog," I cried –
angry little three-year-old terrified
of the dark and the switch,

their farm an alien land,
"and you can't keep me here."
And tried to run away.

So the road would be my way,
destination zero,
for thirty years,
until I came
into the rain.

Forty-odd years have gone in a dream.
And now she is dead.
And I don't quite understand
exactly how to mourn
or how to grieve
over the one who kept the secret
when I was beaten to a scream.

The sun warms my face.
I loved her best from a distance.

The old woman,
as was her way,
calculated everything,
even death, planned everything
down to my ex-
wife's fortune,
and particularly instructed,
"no service, no funeral."

Two cemetery workers, one still

in the high seat of his backhoe,
and the driver of the hearse
who brought her body here,
patiently wait.

Her casket swings
almost imperceptibly
in a faint breeze,
ready to be lowered.

I raise one hand to signal
and the back hoe clangs
and nestles it down
into its gray concrete
sarcophagus, that final resting place.

The workers draw back again.
My daughter steps up alone and drops
a hothouse lily
into the grave. And I step up and drop a rose
and a single sprig of fern.
What my ex contributes
is between herself and the dead.
High clouds burn away.

Her fierce heart demanded,
"No funeral, no service."
She would not cave in
to a Mormon God, would not indulge
the superstitions of her kin.

Rain turned to snow and snow gave way
to sunshine, all in a moment's time.
I step forward again
and present my mudra – *gassho* –
and, whether or not
she approves, recite
the *Nembutsu*,
and bow again, *gassho*,
and clap my hands just once – *good-by* –

good-by to the willow switch that stung my legs
in a life I scarcely remember;
good-by to deceits and denials,
and to all I refuse to forget;
good-by to all she would not hear or speak; good-by
to the grief she willed,
to all the episodes she revised.

In her deathbed, her skin
was tissue-paper thin,
blue veins
like rivulets beneath,
feet cold as February winds.
Her last breaths came
in measured convulsive gasps
with terrible silence between.
And then they stopped.
And that was the end.

I went to stand in the miserable cold
outside the hospital doors

and smoked a cigarette
while they bathed her and dressed her
and brushed her wispy hair into a wave.
Perhaps I wept.

And now she's laid
to rest in frozen ground.
Good-by. I carry the name
of her betrothed, Sam,
but my name
is also Arthur Brown,
as she knew through forty years of lies.

And this prayer or song or summing up
is only the rattle of bones in an orphan's ear,
a talking-to-myself
to ease my fear
as bleak night descends.

And now I turn homeward again,
toward the drone of rain, alone
again at last, in winter light that is gun-metal gray,
familiar chill and ache in my bones.

III.
My old dog is dying.
For a year and more,
I've carried him like a rag
up and down the stairs
as he grew increasingly immobile.
And now he is dying

with all his undying devotion.

When asked, Do dogs
have Buddha-nature?
he answered "Arf!"
who now is dumb,
all rag
and jutting bone and thinning hair,
his half-blue eye
glazed over, brown eye
almost blind.

When he falls,
he cannot rise.

I have carried him out of the house and onto the lawn
to bask in the summer sun,
but his head falls sideways
as he staggers, collapsing
in my lap and slipping
into a coma.

In an hour, he is gone,
head lolled over my leg,
eyes vacant, fierce
loyal heart finally stilled.

And now I scatter his ashes in the woods
beyond this house where we spent sixteen years.

It is summer and rain, and spiders
weave their silver nets

among bamboo leaves
and moss in the garden
breaks into tiny white blossoms.

Evening after evening,
I sit outside
alone,
last hours slipping by,
lost in dying light,

listening to robins sing,
*Twee-dee, tweedly-dee,*
or watching trees grow
or the sky change shape,
destination zero.

So that is what I am.
*Twee-dee, tweedly-dee.*
Whatever the winds forgive, they forgive
with a sigh tonight.
*Twee-dee, tweedly-dee.*
And somehow, that's all right.

IV.
These narrow highways plunge through tiny mining towns
vanishing under Colorado mountains,
they draw a thread
across impossible deserts
or split the rolling hills of Iowa farms
no one will remember
except for a moment's regret.

Burying our dead, we write out our lives
in disappearing ink, the landscape sliding by
just outside the window, the lost lake
of childhood followed hard by the granite
cliffs of divorce, and before you know it,
there's nothing left but photographs
slightly out of focus, a vague visual note
about tamaracks painting valleys
somewhere west of Missoula
in what-the-hell-year-was-that,
and Don't-you-remember
is a game for passing hours.

Somewhere between Truth
Or Consequences, New Mexico,
and the Indian school in Browning,
history slips silently by,
leaving only its poisoned blankets.
The buffalo hunters are all gone
and the log trucks are permanently parked
outside the Cascade Cafe
where philosophy is free
and grim and the paint
is stained from leaks. Bad coffee
comes cheap and there's a simple solution
for everything under the sun.

You stop for gas in Barstow or Nogales
and the sky turns blazing orange.
You scrape the bugs from your windshield
and slip back onto a road

running straight into the darkness,
an old tune summoning a time
when you still loved – was it –
your second wife
and kids clung to your knees.
Now they are grown.
But all that falls away behind the glare
of headlights on a hill or a passing cattle-car,
erased by the steady whine of wheels.

You drive through Boise, Butte, or Blaine,
coffee in Nisqually, a truck stop john in Ellensburg
or Drain. By midnight,
they all smell the same, urine,
tar and oil and diesel exhaust, and coffee
that tastes of styrofoam.

On the loneliest bleak nights
in the heart of the American west,
you can drive all night forever
and no matter how far you get,
you wake up again in the west,
the landscape constantly changing,
but always so vast that
everyone is alone and history is a bad
novel you can close
whenever you need a good night's sleep
or the general oblivion of Holiday Inn.

Then the meadowlark sings up first light. Or you hear
the mockingbird

or a mourning dove and know
it is a desert at your feet, the road
already dancing in the heat,
distant hills transparent, shimmering in waves.

Or a tired hawk
scowls from his perch on a split-rail fence, then rises
on effortless wings, crucified against the sky,
high damp mountain air
carrying the odor of ammonia
up from the pasture below.
Up the last canyons,
crossing over the Great Divide,
there will be snow.

v.
In the middle of the afternoon, my paramour
pauses with her wheelbarrow load
of freshly dug iris bulbs
destined for the compost heap
and asks, What now.

"Simplify. Simplify."
I repeat it like a mantra, "Simplify."
I do not despise my ex-wife's
iris nor her foxglove nor her plague
of wild violets, but they must go.

Here, I'll plant a lace-leaf maple;
there, a Japanese iris and a pale lily
in a bed of moss in the shade. The rose

was eaten by passing deer, but its stubble
will remain and grow.

Prune the English ivy, the clematis,
and this thorny stuff that grows along the wall.
Dig out the weeping cherry and cut a wide path
through the turf leading to the studio we'll build.
We'll buck six cords of wood from the trees we fell.

And as evening comes on, we pause again together.
The slash pile crackles and smokes.
Somewhere in the dusk a few frogs
begin to sing frog-love songs.
Rivulets of sweat run down Gray's face as she grins.

Her shirt, knotted below her breasts,
is plastered to her chest.
High overhead, a nighthawk darts and cries.
I open her shirt and we stretch
our aching bodies in the grass to cool.

Another sun drowns in the west. A wall
of light fog descends through the woods,
pushing inland from the strait. I roll on my side
and inch slowly down her body, kissing
her breasts and belly, and lay my head on her thigh.

A few feet away, at the edge of the grass,
a salamander moves even more slowly
into shadows beneath a rotting cedar stump.
A faint breeze raises goose-bumps

on Gray's damp skin

and makes her nipples pucker.
I rise and cover her body
with my body, hugging her hard for warmth.
She tastes of salt and longing.
And we lie naked in our garden,

sweaty and chilly, exhausted,
and make lazy love against the night
while the first faint stars come on
like porch lights blinking down a highway
unwinding a timeless river.

VI.

As if the water would answer, I go on talking.
I am telling the waves the story of my days,
I am entering my plea at the tribunal of the sea,
walking alone along the shore at Kalaloch.

Here I once made love with a woman I adored
while a lonely figure watched from bluffs high above,
and the gray implacable tide drew away
to meet the gray implacable sky.

Our cries – love or death – were drowned
by the cries of wandering gulls. Now a year
has passed. And still he is there, watching
from the shadows, sighing the sighs of the sea.

Memory, like waves. Stained with the salts of desire,

a shoreline creature talking fear away,
I go on confessing to the water, understanding
only that the final sentence is death,

a mist falling over the moon,
that is the signature of all things,
beautiful and empty
as the solitary seed syllable of the loon.

# Elegy

It is almost dawn,
the procession of stars
journeying again
into blindness. You who could
not touch me show me the way.

# Old Bones

## I

All the quiet afternoon splitting wood,
thinking about books, I remembered

Snyder making a handle for an ax
as he remembered Ezra Pound

thirty years before,
thinking about Lu Chi.

Using the ax, I forget the ax.
Closing my eyes, I see.

II.
Thirty-one new yellow daffodils
bloom in the little garden.

Alder seed covers everything
with little flakes of rust.

A breeze through evergreens.
Distant bird-trills.

When Hui Neng tore up the sutras,
his bones were already dust.

III.
Wanting one good organic line,
I wrote a thousand sonnets.

Wanting a little peace,
I folded a thousand cranes.

Every discipline a new evasion;
every crane a dodge:

Bashō didn't know a thing about water
until he heard the frog.

# Another Duffer

"The poem is the cry of its occasion,
Part of the *res* itself and not about it."
The poem speaks the poet.

Just as you, head steady as a rock,
let the left shoulder drop
unnaturally, arms brought

back extended, so that
what the body most becomes
is a pendulum,

and the clear smooth arc
of the ball leaves no mark
across the sky and the eye

must lift too late to see –
beginning to foregone conclusion –
what the mind already perceives

accurately, in perfect detail: poem:
like the man and the club and the turf and the ball in golf,
like your finger and the moon, like the water and the whale,

like three or four brands of Zen,
various music of singer and song, –
*is, – are, – will be, – has been,* –
and, finally, *am.*

## Sonnet

I would not call my love a red, red rose,
but a common thing, a dandelion
sprung suddenly up among the rubble
and thistle, there among the iron scraps
rusting in the rain – a common flower
or weed blossoming among the refuse
of this world, only then to be scattered
in the emptiness by evening winds.

Let my love for you be the least of things,
the evening breeze itself, ever-present,
almost unnoticed in its constancy.
As it is for me – as whole, natural
as the drawing of a breath. Any less
is nothing; any more, superfluous.

# Cooking

The powerful aroma of hot olive oil,
basil, and a double-pinch of cayenne
for cooking mushrooms and green onions –
skillet about to smoke, I'm cooking for you again,

and, outside, the pungent odor of rain,
rain rapping windows like tiny fingers drumming.
Oil slides away toward the skillet's edge
and cackles when I dump the onions in.

In the oven, a salmon bakes in a brew
of butter, garlic, and wine. Coltrane's
cooking his way through *Olé*
on the box, blowing ineffably toward that hot

bass duet, and oh, don't I remember how
beautiful you were that sweltering
summer day, bare skinned, melon juice
running down your chin, and you're still not

here yet.

# *Jubilate Sutra*

> "I mean, graces come slowly..."
>     – ROBERT CREELEY

For I will consider the graces of this woman
for she is comely,
for the graces come slowly and she has been patient,
for hers are the graces of a woman who is daughter-sister-
    lover-mother-grandmother,
for she is a woman,
for she has known men and has lain with them, loved them,
    and made progeny;
for she raised her children alone when her husbands proved
    abusive,
for she mothered her children when their fathers moved on,
for she is a mother,
for she loved them and taught them;
for she has made shelter for battered women,
for she has made shelter for children;
for she has been mother to many
for she has loved men who were children,
for she has loved and forgiven,
for her graces are earned more than given,
for she has given the gift of herself to many,
for she has aided the battered and the batterer alike, fed the
    hungry, and asked for nothing,
for she is comely.

For she has found truth in poetry,

for her ears have heard Levertov, Rich, and Carruth, Creeley
    and Whitman,
for she loves Lee's porcine legacies and Snyder's mountains,
for she loves Laux and Lao Tzu and Sappho and more,
for she reads thriller novels and loves trashy movies,
for she knows how the Graces sing,
for she can sing the blues and drink tequila,
for she loves Bobby Bland, Etta James, George Jones, and Hank
    Crawford,
for she can hum to Nina Simone or sway in a trance to a
    Coltrane tune,
for she can listen and she can sing
for she knows the difference,
for she knows what happens when the two come together,
for her wisdom is funky,
for she has held the brush in hand and seen it fail and seen it
    succeed
for she has eyes to see,
for she has seen within herself the terror and did not turn away
for she has eyes that have seen the world
for she has passed through tenements of hopelessness and pity,
for her wisdom is funky:

for she knows the difference between washing and not washing
    dishes
is not the difference between washing and not washing dishes
for she is wise with the wisdom of family, pregnant with
    meaning,
for she has changed a grandchild's diaper and remembered
    from whence we come,
for she finds pleasure in the daily and

for her, pleasures are small but many,
for this is her signature of affection,
for she can buck wood and plant irises in the garden,
for she feeds blue jays all winter and finches in springtime,
for she listens for the nighthawk on the early summer dusk,
for she has watched the sky long after the passing of wild
     ducks on an autumn afternoon,
for she has made love in the garden in sunlight, laughing,
for she loves for me to undress her or to dress her
for she loves to tease and to play,
for she loves erotic stories, politics and philosophy,
for she is curious and sometimes angry,
for delight is her teacher,
for her heart is often overcome with joy,
for it is comely.

For she is the figure of mercy,
for she is the daughter-sister-mother, perfect in her
     imperfections,
for she is grandmother's wisdom, foolish and wise and
     mortal,
for the lines in her face are a map of the graces,
for her laughter is clearer than water;
for her laughter dances like candlelight, like moonlight
     through branches,
for her laughter is warmer than fire,
for her laughter is clearer than water,
for I feed her spicy prawns, cream cheese with jalapeño jelly,
for she kisses and licks my fingers,
for I feed her ice cream and brandy after dinner,
for I heat her saké and pour cup after cup

for her appetites are deserving, my fondest pleasure,
for she is a light in the darkness of my days,
for she is the spark that ignites the fire that warms my bed
at night,
for her body is warmer than mine, it is a fire,
for she turns in her sleep and drags the sheets from the bed
for she is a furnace,
for I hug her for warmth,
for her body's a furnace and I am dark, hard as coal,
for the fire rages but the embers never perish,
for she is comely;

for she is my sister, my companion,
for I confide in her as in no other,
for we have no secrets,
for she honors all the women I have loved in all my days –
daughter, sister, mother –
for the graces come slowly, but hers are many,
for I love her as she is and so love her more for having loved
others before me,
for she is wise with her learning,
for I tell her the secrets of erotic dreams to arouse her,
for she tells me,
for she has loved and learned with every day and given what
she could
for her generosity is boundless,
for she has brought me the many splendors of her mind
and body
for she has mastered the arts of compassion and
for we have mastered the arts of poverty of all but affection,
for she has loved being in love with men,

for she has loved women also, and stood by them in
    friendship,
for she has loved children with a mother's love
for she has seen them grown and seen some destroyed and
    seen her children's children,
for she has loved them all, her own and others'
for she has learned a patience that is a grace;
for she has dried my tears and wiped the fever from my face,
for she has made my life her life and her life mine,
for she is the figure of mercy, and gentle;

for her appetite in bed is enormous
for she has learned to whisper her each desire
for she asks me to please her,
for she has made love with multitudes in the chambers of
    our dreams,
for her fingers map the geography of pleasure in my body;
for her sighs are holy,
for her ecstasy is my ecstasy when I touch her or taste her
for we have made the twin-backed beast and heard it scream
    and made it purr
for I am a cat in her lap, Sappho's sparrow drinking long at
    her fountain,
for her sighs are holy,
for she is a mountain when she shudders
for she welcomes me to deep rivers and dark forests
for she is a mountain and an ocean and I am a seeker,
for she is a journey, not destination,
for she is the one who draws me out, toward,
for she is my muse as we stand folding laundry,
for her, I brew Sunday latte

for she is lovely naked in my bed
for her hair is tangled like the threads of our love and our lives,
for she smells of the salts of desire and the sugars of wisdom
for we have worked hard in the garden together,
for we have made love through many dark hours,
for I will lick her body and taste our afterlove and sweat and
    sing hosanna
for I will draw her bath water
for I will wash her back and feet
for she is the song and the thread that binds,
for she is sister-lover, dearest companion,
for she is most comely;

for her lips, I come bearing kisses,
for her eyes, I come bearing kisses, and
for all the subtleties of throat and thigh and breast and knee, I
    come with kisses,
for her finger, I come bearing a ring and a promise;

for she is modest, embarrassed by my praises,
for she will blush when I compare her nipples to the rosebud,
for she may allow a stranger to glimpse them during loveplay
for she is brave and adores her own imagination
for she loves being loved
for she loves to dream and play and imagine,
for she has borne pain and has learned,
for she has braved fear and has learned,
for she has braved love and has learned,
for she has scars and wounds,
for I am her poultice;

for she is my teacher and I listen;
for she has made me the object of her desire,
for she has shown me to be foolish and mawkish;
for she has clothed me in the blankets of devotion;
for she has given me what I could not give myself;
for she is comely.

For she is patient, she has learned that graces come slowly.
For I adore her, I sing her praises most highly.
For I am grateful, her love makes me humble.
For I am grateful, her love makes me humble.

## What the Water Knows

What the mouth sings, the soul must learn to forgive.
A rat's as moral as a monk in the eyes of the real world.
Still, the heart is a river
pouring from itself, a river that cannot be crossed.

It opens on a bay
and turns back upon itself as the tide comes in,
it carries the cry of the loon and the salts
of the unutterably human.

A distant eagle enters the mouth of a river
salmon no longer run and his wide wings glide
upstream until he disappears
into the nothing from which he came. Only the thought
    remains.

Lacking the eagle's cunning or the wisdom of the sparrow,
where shall I turn, drowning in sorrow?
Who will know what the trees know, the spidery patience
of young maple or what the willows confess?

Let me be water. The heart pours out in waves.
Listen to what the water says.
Wind, be a friend.
There's nothing I couldn't forgive.

# A NOTE ON THE POEMS

The earliest drafts and lines of these poems date from
the mid-sixties, the earliest publication coming circa
1972. I have revised many of the poems for this edition
and present them in roughly chronological order but for
the prefatory "A Lover's Quarrel," written ca. 1985, and
have included selections from all of my published vol-
umes of poetry except the book-length *Triada*. Alas, I've
not been a tidy bibliographer, and therefore extend
sincere apologies to any editors or journals I may have
carelessly omitted from the acknowledgments.

SAM HAMILL was born in the spring of 1943, probably somewhere in northern California. His father, an itinerate illiterate World War II veteran, left him, ca. 1972, with an agency in northern Utah with instructions that he be adopted by someone who would teach him to read and write. Adopted by a Utah farm family, he left school to live on the streets during the Beat heyday of the late fifties. He served four years in the U.S. Marine Corps, much of it in Japan, where he became a Conscientious Objector. He attended L.A. Valley College and the University of California, Santa Barbara, on the GI Bill. Since founding Copper Canyon Press in 1972, he has taught in prisons for thirteen years and in artists-in-education programs for nearly twenty years, and has published more than thirty books, including translations from classical Chinese, Japanese, ancient Greek, Latin, and Estonian poetry, three volumes of essays, and a dozen volumes of original poetry. He is contributing editor at *American Poetry Review* and at *Tricycle: The Buddhist Review*, and has been the recipient of fellowships from the National Endowment for the Arts, the Guggenheim Foundation, the U.S.–Japan Friendship Commission, and the Lila Wallace–Reader's Digest Foundation. He lives near Port Townsend, Washington.